RESCUED ME

RESCUED ME
NESTOR "THE BOSS" GOMEZ

TORTOISE BOOKS
CHICAGO

TABLE OF CONTENTS

This book is dedicated to all my friends
(the four-legged kind)
and to sweet Mel, my wife,
who reignited my love for life.

Warning:
This book might cause the reader to feel an uncontrollable urge to adopt a dog or cat.
The author hereby accepts your everlasting thanks.

DANCE CONTEST

I met the woman who would become my second wife at a Latin music club; we fell in love dancing to the rhythms of Mexican cumbia. From then on when she and I went out, we usually went cumbia dancing. And when I say we went out, I mean we went out!

We often got to the club at 11 PM on Friday night and didn't leave until 5 AM the next morning. Then, on Saturday night, we were back at the club by 11 PM and again didn't leave until 5 AM on Sunday. Finally, on Sunday, we got to the club at the same time as the previous two nights and left the club only after it closed. Then we went straight home, took a shower, and from there went to work.

Like I said, we went out.

We lived like that for a few years.

Then I found out she had been cheating on me...and after a long, nasty, and messy divorce, whenever I went cumbia dancing, the place, the people, and the music reminded me of my cheating ex-wife. I needed to purge my body, mind, and soul of her memory.

But I loved dancing.

So I decided to switch to dancing salsa instead of cumbia. Now, those of you who are not familiar with Latin music must be wondering: cumbia, salsa, aren't those the same?

No, they are not.

Imagine that you grew up playing American football, and then in college you decided to start playing *futbol* instead. It is still a sport, played on a field with a goal, but the ball, the rules, and even the people watching are completely different.

Still I thought it would be easy to switch. I told myself: "How hard can it be? I am Latino; this music is in my veins."

One of the first nights I went salsa dancing, I met a young lady, and we became friends. I needed to learn to dance salsa to forget my ex-wife; she needed to learn because her boyfriend was an amazing dancer, and also a jerk who didn't want to dance with her because she didn't know how to dance.

After months of going to the salsa clubs, I had only been able to learn a few basic steps.

Meanwhile, my lady friend had learned a lot.

"Wow, you have gotten really good. Did your boyfriend teach you?" I asked her, after seeing all her sexy moves.

"No, the jerk never wants to teach me. I have been taking salsa classes," she replied.

I am cheap. I didn't want to pay for salsa classes. But after weeks of making slow progress in the free salsa lessons at the salsa clubs, I gave up and decided to spend a little bit of money. I followed my friend's suggestion and I enrolled in salsa classes at the dance school.

There I met many people who are still my friends to this day—among them a Mexican ballerina, a professional dancer who had recently emigrated from Mexico. She didn't know any English, and was there to meet people and to learn salsa.

One day, jokingly, I asked the ballerina to be my partner in the upcoming salsa contest that the dance school was putting together. To my surprise, she agreed.

We spent months practicing. We put together a choreographed dance number that had complicated turns, sexy moves, and a lift like in the movie *Dirty Dancing*.

The night of the contest, my lady friend came to show her support for us. She was just about to leave when she saw that the jerk, who by now was her ex-boyfriend, was also there.

I didn't want her to leave. "Don't worry," I told her "The ballerina and I are going to kick his ass on the dance floor."

She agreed to stay.

When the music started, me, the ballerina, and the other couples in the competition started dancing.

The only one who wasn't dancing was the jerk. He was waiting for his partner, who was running late.

I was dancing when suddenly I forgot everything. I froze in the middle of the dance floor.

"*Muevete.* Just move," the ballerina said, grabbing my hand. I pretended to dance while she moved graciously around me. I looked over at the jerk, who was now dancing with his partner, and they were amazing. When the song ended, I walked off the dance floor feeling defeated.

I walked to the bar to get a drink and ordered a Long Island Iced Tea. And then, since I was still thirsty, I ordered a second one. And since those two tasted good, I ordered a third one.

After all, I was sure we had gotten eliminated from the competition.

That's when I heard the judges calling the ballerina and I back to the dance floor for the next round.

But this time maybe because I thought we had already lost, or maybe due to the Long Island Iced Teas, I did not forget anything. I did the complicated turns and the sexy moves, and the lift with only one hand.

In the end, we placed second, and the best part was that the jerk did not place.

"Did you see that?" I asked my lady friend when the contest ended.

"Yes, you got second place," she responded.

"Not that. We beat your ex. We beat the jerk," I said, excited. And then before I could stop myself, I added, "I love you."

For a long minute, she didn't say anything.

Finally, she looked at me and said, "I love you too."

(It must have been my sexy moves.)

ROOMMATES

The first time I went to see my new girlfriend at her place, I wanted to make a good impression. After all, we were about to take our relationship to a new level.

Dressed in my Sunday best, I stood in front of her door trying to look as assertive and confident as I could.

I knocked, and after a few seconds she opened the door.

That's when her seventy-pound, scary, muscular pit-bull mix started barking at me.

Immediately, I jumped back and started screaming, "Please put your dog away!!!"

I was terrified of dogs.

When I was a ten-year-old kid living in Guatemala, I had gone to a neighbor's house on an errand. I'd knocked on the door, and a few seconds later I heard my neighbor approaching the door. My neighbor opened the door, but before I could say a single word her dog squeezed through the little gap and bit me in my thigh. Where on the thigh? Let's just say that if the dog had bit me a few inches higher, my life would have been forever transformed.

From that day forward I developed an extreme fear of dogs.

I became the guy that would not enter a house or a room if a dog was present. If I was outside, I would cross the street if I saw a dog walking on my side of the street.

I knew that my new girlfriend had roommates—and by roommates, I mean her dog and two cats—but I didn't expect to see such a big and muscular pit bull barking at me the moment she opened the door. I know now that he was just trying to protect her, but at that time I felt that he was telling me I was not welcome there.

The next time I visited her, she locked her dog in a room. Meanwhile her cats sat on the windowsills—the female cat ignoring me, the male cat watching me the whole time.

But locking the dog away didn't last too long.

One day I came to my girlfriend's house and she refused to lock her dog away. "You have to get used to him," she said.

I felt that it was her dog that needed to get used to me.

"Maybe you should come with me when I walk him," my girlfriend suggested.

That's how Sunday morning walks became a ritual for us.

We walked to the nearest restaurant. One of us, usually her, stayed outside with the dog while the other one would order two coffees and two sandwiches. Then we walked to the nearest park so her dog could run around while we enjoyed our breakfast.

But most times, her dog would stay close to us while we ate. My girlfriend would eat her breakfast, immune to the puppy eyes her dog made while begging for scraps. To my surprise I found myself easy prey to his whines.

At first, I cut small pieces of my sandwich to share with her dog. Then I started buying fries or hashbrowns to feed to him, until I eventually started adding a sandwich for the dog to our weekly breakfast order.

The sharing of food brought her dog and me closer, so much that I eventually started to take him out on walks by myself (although once or twice I might have contemplated the idea of letting go of the leash and pretending he had run away).

My girlfriend would always remind me: "Be careful when another dog walks nearby; he doesn't get along with other dogs."

And: "Don't take him into a dog park, and never take off his leash."

And: "Don't let him eat food off the sidewalk, but if he starts eating something don't try to take it away."

Each of those warnings did little to ease my still-present fear of dogs.

When I first heard those warnings, I asked her, "Did you mean to adopt the scariest dog you could find?"

She proceeded to recount the story of how she had come to meet her dog.

Back in the days when I was still trying to learn to dance salsa, my girlfriend had decided to adopt a dog. In fact, she had fallen in love with a dog that she saw every weekend at the dog shelter across the street from the salsa school where she took lessons.

But there was a small problem.

That dog wasn't a dog fit to live in an apartment. He barked too much and had too much energy; therefore, the dog needed a lot of space. He needed to be adopted into a home. So my girlfriend had come up with a brilliant plan.

She asked her aunt, a homeowner, to adopt the dog for her—with the understanding that her aunt was only going to sign the papers, and my girlfriend was going to be the one to take the dog into her apartment.

It took a while for her aunt to agree to the plan.

By the time they came back to the shelter to adopt the dog, he had already been adopted by a family in the suburbs. Heartbreak is not a strong enough word to describe how my girlfriend felt.

She left the dog shelter in tears.

Many days later, she pushed herself to start searching for another dog.

She found a dog up for adoption and she went to see him.

Online, they had claimed that he was under 50 lbs and got along with other dogs.

But upon meeting the dog, she realized that he was bigger and that there were caution signs all over his crate.

No toys in his crate.

No blankets.

Don't take out with other dogs.

Still, she decided to take a chance. She took a tennis ball that was lying nearby and threw it at him. He caught it in his mouth and ripped it in two pieces in seconds, then brought it back to her.

Fearing that he might try to do the same thing to her cats, she asked: "Is he friendly with cats?"

They assured her that he had passed a cat test. (Although they didn't bother to explain what the test had entailed.)

There was something about him that drew her to him. When the shelter offered to forgo the adoption fee, she decided to take a chance on him.

"Did you mean to adopt the scariest-looking dog you could find?" her friends and aunt asked when they saw her dog for the first time.

"He is actually very loving and friendly, once he approves of you," she would explain them. She would add that he got along with her cats.

At first I had felt the same thing as everyone else, that my girlfriend had adopted the scariest-looking dog she could find. But I eventually had to agree with her that her dog was in fact very loving and kind. Well, at least with her. Not so much with other dogs, or cats that dared to cross his path as we walked.

Eventually I started to win her dog's approval by sharing not only my Sunday sandwich with him, but also my everyday meals. I started to take small portions of my plate and feed them to him as I ate.

Before I knew it, sharing my meal had become a bonding experience for us. I learned not to be too afraid of him—first by placing food on the floor near him to eat, and eventually graduating to feeding him off the palm of my hand.

He must have learned that I would feed him whenever I had food, and I guess that he must have decided that was a good enough reason to tolerate having me around.

EVIL

Soon the cats started to join in the meal-sharing moments.

The female cat would eat the pieces of food that I shared with her and then jump back to her spot by the window. But the male cat was demanding; he would stare at me if I took too long to feed him. That cat soon proved difficult to live with. He walked around like he owned the place, pushing everyone out of the way. I started to believe that my girlfriend's two other roommates were afraid of him.

The worst thing about the male cat was that during dinner, he loved to help himself to other people's food, even mine. I usually looked the other way when he stole food right off my plate, not because I was afraid of him; I just wanted to keep the peace.

One day I came to my girlfriend's place to surprise her. I had stopped by her favorite restaurant and picked up some of her favorite food. The first thing I did when I got to her place was to have a talk with her roommates. I explained to them my plan and I asked them to please stay away from the dining room so me and my girl could have some time alone.

They seemed to understand me, and I got the place ready: candlelight, romantic music, some roses, wine, and her favorite food set up on the table for when she came home from work.

She loved the surprise, and after she put her work stuff away, she sat down to have a nice romantic dinner with me. But then out of the corner of my eye I saw the male cat sneaking into the dining room. I tried to ignore him, but then I saw him reaching for my plate.

I pushed him and screamed at him to get out of the room.

The male cat was pissed and looked at me as if ready to kill me, but then he turned around and left.

"I'm sorry..." I started to tell my girlfriend, wanting to apologize for screaming at her cat, but then out of the corner of my eye I caught him going into the bedroom.

But just as fast as he went in, he came out.

That seemed very strange to me, so I excused myself from the table and went to the bedroom to see what the evil cat had been up to. That's when I discovered my favorite jacket laying on the floor with a big wet spot right in the middle of it.

He had peed on my jacket.

This was no accident; this was a declaration of war. I readied myself for battle, knowing that to win this war I would have to play it cool and let my superior intellect guide me to victory.

I went back to the kitchen and acted as if nothing was wrong.

Hours later, my girlfriend and I went to sleep.

I lay awake in bed, waiting for everyone to fall asleep. When I thought the moment was right, I got up as if I was going to the washroom, but I headed for the living room instead. There on the sofa was the evil cat, sleeping.

I stood in front of the sofa and I unzipped my pants, ready to pee all over him.

But at the last moment I realized that I wasn't going to be able to explain to my girlfriend why I had been peeing in the living room. And what's more, the cat was probably going to wake up and start making a lot of noise, which meant the dog would wake up, freak out, and either start to bark or jump at me and bite me.

So I decided to go back to bed instead.

I quickly fell asleep, but I awoke a few hours later with the feeling that I was being watched. I opened my eyes, and I discovered the evil cat sitting on my chest.

He was staring down at me with an evil grin on his face. He had snuck into the bedroom in the middle of the night, and now he was probably going to kill me, somehow.

There was nothing left for me to do, so I closed my eyes and hoped for a quick death.

After a while, I opened my eyes to discover that he was gone.

I couldn't go back to sleep that night, and, early in the morning as soon as my girlfriend woke up, I made an excuse to get out of there.

It's strange because I had always been afraid of dogs, especially pit bulls, but I was more or less getting along with my girlfriend's dog now. And it's even stranger that I had never had problems with cats before. I didn't have trouble with the female cat, but the male cat, that evil cat, I just didn't seem to get along with that cat...

PELO EN LA SOPA

After the incident with her cat, I started to spend fewer nights at my girlfriend's place. Instead, I started to tell her, "Bring your dog over to my place." That way I felt that she wouldn't feel bad for leaving him alone at her place when she came to visit me, and I wouldn't have to deal with her evil cat.

The nights that she agreed to bring her dog over, I placed a blanket at the foot of my bed so he could sleep close to us without leaving hair all over my bed. Still, the first couple of nights that she brought him over, I slept with one eye open, afraid that he would suddenly wake up, forget that he was sleeping over at my place, and attack me in the middle of the night.

The one benefit of having her dog there was that she didn't have to wake up early and rush out of my place to go to her place to walk her dog and feed her cats. She could sleep late at my place and walk him on her way back to her apartment, and the cats didn't mind eating late. The one inconvenience was finding dog hair all over my place the next day.

That was the one thing, besides her cat, that I didn't like about her place: I often found dog hair all over the sofa, the carpet, the floor: everywhere.

For years, I had seen people at work, on the train, or at the coffee shop who were walking around with their clothes covered in their pet's hair. They seemed to be unaware, or worse: they didn't care.

I didn't want to be one of those people. That was a huge *pelo en la sopa* for me. (*Hair in the soup*, a Spanish phrase meaning there's a problem in a situation.)

But even more obvious than the dog hair was the bond between my girlfriend and her pets. In most of Latin America, cats are predominantly used to get rid of vermin like rats and mice. Dogs are mainly used as a form of protecting the house from intruders. Perhaps, as a single woman, my girlfriend had at first adopted her cats as companions and her dog as a form of protection, but she treated them more like members of her family than pets.

Then again they got along perfectly without me; it was me—with my fear and my preconceived notions of how a pet should be treated—that was bringing chaos into her household.

So maybe it was me who was *el pelo en la sopa*.

GOOD NIGHT

I might have reached a level of self-awareness that was not familiar to me, but it was quickly discarded the next day when I went to her place, sat on the sofa, and was instantly covered by dog and cat hair.

Annoyed, I got up from the sofa and went to the only piece of furniture where I could sit down to read a book and not be covered by dog hair: my girlfriend's bed.

But I couldn't sit on the bed; in fact, I often found myself unable to sleep in the bed.

My girlfriend's bed could only be described as a bed of nails. Then again, an actual bed of nails might have been more comfortable, and safer.

On first look it seemed just like any other normal bed, but as soon as one's body made contact with the mattress, one could see that it was a very old bed, whose springs had long ago stopped working properly.

Many times, while sleeping at her place, I was awakened in the middle of the night by the pain of a broken spring stabbing me in the back, or the ass. I feared I would one night roll over in my sleep and suddenly lose an eye or get stabbed in the neck by the sharpened edge of a spring.

"How can anyone sleep in this bed?" I asked myself one night, and glanced at the figure of my girlfriend contorted across the only section of the bed that still had semi-functioning springs.

I wanted to ask her to switch places with me, but I decided against it. I tend to move a lot in my sleep anyway, and I didn't think I would be comfortable forcing my body to mold into the small space free of broken springs.

The next morning, I asked her, "Why don't you get a new bed?"

She looked at me in surprise. "I can't get rid of the bed; it was gifted to me."

Curious, I asked, "Gifted by who?"

"My dad," she responded, and then she added almost casually, "It used to belong to him."

Now it was I who was surprised. "You mean to tell me that used to be your parents' bed?"

"Sure," she responded. "But my sister also used it for a few years." She said that as if it would make things better, instead of worse.

Suddenly that bed was not only as dangerous as a bed of nails, it was also awkward. It felt wrong to sleep there.

I knew that family was important to her and that she kept some furniture that used to belong to her grandmother, her sisters, and her aunt. It was kind of sweet—endearing even; I loved that about her. My family had left everything we owned behind when we emigrated to Chicago. I felt both jealousy and admiration that she owned and valued some of her family heirlooms. But only if those furniture heirlooms were a desk, a table, or even glassware. A bed, especially one previously owned by her parents—that was another thing altogether.

I decided to take matters into my own hands and surprised her by buying her a bed.

But a new bed is expensive, and I am kind of cheap.

So instead, I started to search the internet for a used bed.

I figured that she was already sleeping in a used bed anyway. And as long as the bed that I bought had working springs and didn't belong to her parents or mine, it would be an improvement.

I was in luck. I found a set of mattresses so cheap it was kind of a giveaway. And they were practically new. A groom-to-be had purchased his soon-to-be bride a new set, but when she learned that they were of the memory foam kind, she had made him return them. But he had purchased them during a sale, the kind of *no-refunds-no-returns* sale.

Now, he just wanted somebody to take them off his hands.

In fact, he was so glad that I was buying them that he threw in a headboard and a bed frame as well.

"What are you doing?" my girlfriend asked a couple of hours later, when I showed up at her apartment.

"It's a surprise." I started to carry her old bed down the stairs.

I put the old mattress in the alley (but not before one of the broken springs pricked me for one last time) and I brought the new bed upstairs.

I could hear that she was upset when she said, "I didn't ask you for that."

"I know. I told you it was a surprise." I took her by the hand and asked her to sit on the bed.

Her dog walked into the bedroom, looked at me and at the bed, and then looked away, as if to tell me that he wasn't impressed either.

I tried to ignore him and instead I told my girlfriend: "Lay down. Feel how soft it is." Her dog jumped in the bed as if I had told him to lay down and cuddle up next to her. Next thing I knew, her cats had come into the room and joined the party.

I wanted to tell her cats and dog to get down from the bed, but I was running late for work and I didn't want to make my girlfriend madder.

The next day I came over to see how she liked the new bed.

I noticed that she had bought a new set of blankets for it.

"Hey, I got you a new blanket too," I said, showing the heating blanket I had gotten at the store.

She gave the blanket a disapproving look.

"I get really cold in winter," I said. "Heating blankets are the best."

"I'm afraid my dog might chew on it," she said, while putting the heating blanket away inside a closet.

And then she said those words every man fears: "We need to talk."

I prepared for the worst; it didn't take long.

"So where is this relationship going?" my girlfriend asked.

"What do you mean?" I asked, although I knew exactly what she meant.

She pointed at the bed. "You just brough me a bed."

I pointed out the obvious. "You needed one."

"Are we going to continue having sleepovers, or will we ever move in together?"

I looked at her and asked, "How old is your dog?"

Shocked at my question, she responded, "What does that have to do with anything?"

"Well," I responded, "we are not moving in together until your dog dies."

Not surprisingly, she got really mad at me.

Even after I reminded her of my childhood fear of dogs.

Even after a couple of days. Even after a couple of weeks. She was still mad at me.

It seemed that our relationship was coming to an end.

One night she called me, and when I answered the phone she seemed very upset.

"I am throwing out your bed; come to the alley to pick it up."

I had no idea how she was going to do that by herself, but I didn't question her, nor did I get upset.

I had a fever; I was feeling too sick to argue. Instead I said, "Don't do anything tonight; please think it over and let us talk in the morning."

We said goodnight and avoided a fight.

Early the next day she came to my place. I was still feeling sick; I had spent the night on the sofa, unable to sleep in my own bed.

She cuddled up next to me.

I asked, "Did you throw the bed away?"

"I wasn't really going to; I was just upset," she replied.

I looked at her. "I'm glad you didn't get rid of it."

"I actually like it a lot. It's so cozy." She gave me a little kiss. "Thank you."

"Well, even this old sofa is cozy compared to your old bed. I just wish you wouldn't let your pets in it."

She got serious again: "They are not just my pets; they are part of my family. If you want to have a life with me, that has to include them as well."

This was a do-or-die kind of thing. My refusal to accept her pets was the *pelo en la sopa* of our relationship. This could put an end to an otherwise-perfect relationship. It was not enough of me to tolerate her pets. I needed to learn to live with them.

After that conversation, I started once again to try to make peace with her pets.

I once again started to try to get close to her dog and cats.

But I didn't get a chance to make peace with her male cat.

He was really old and one day he simply ran out of time. My girlfriend was sad. I drove her to the closest veterinarian to have him euthanized. I also felt sad for the old guy. In a strange kind of way, he had earned my respect.

After that experience, my girlfriend and I decided to stop wasting time and move in together.

But even without her male cat, we knew that my place was too small for all of us. Her place was bigger, but the building where she rented had just gotten sold, and the new owner was planning to increase the already-too-high rent.

We figured that instead of paying high rent, we could combine our salaries and savings and look for an affordable place we could buy together.

"The two things I want," my girlfriend said, "are to find a place where my dog and cat are welcome, and that is close to my mom."

I agreed, since my mother lived close to her mother's house and I also wanted to stay close to my mother.

I assured my girlfriend, "Surely we can find something right away."

But after a quick search on Google, we realized that real estate is a dog-eat-dog kind of world. We were going to need some help.

My girlfriend contacted a friend who happened to be a real estate agent, and we started the search for our dream place.

Sadly, we couldn't find anything near our moms' neighborhoods that we could afford. We decided to extend our search to nearby neighborhoods.

But most places were either too expensive, or required too much work and repairs.

The few that were OK and my girlfriend liked, I wasn't happy with. And when we found a place I liked, my girlfriend did not agree with me. The couple of times we agreed on a place, they either didn't accept dogs, or the taxes were too high, or someone else put in a higher bid than ours.

After about six months of search, during which we visited hundreds of places, we were fighting like cats and dogs.

"Just tell me you don't want to live with me," I told my girlfriend one day as we argued over yet another place.

"It's you who doesn't want to live with my dog," she reminded me. "Maybe we should just rent a place."

"I don't want to rent," I said. "I want to find our dream place"

"Fine," she said. "Where is your dream place?"

I had not thought about that. I had been too worried about finding a place we could afford that was close to our mothers and that accepted her pit bull that I hadn't thought about what I really wanted. But when I did, I told her:

"When my family came to Chicago, we lived in Uptown near the lake. I loved it there. After that, I moved so many times I ended up living all over the city, but I always missed being near the lake."

"What"? my girlfriend said angrily. "We have not looked at anything close to the lake."

The next day she found a listing for a two-bedroom place in Edgewater.

"It's one block from the train, one block from Lake Shore Drive, one block from the lake, and five minutes from your job," she said when she told me about it.

I was sure it was going to be another disappointing viewing, but I went to see the place with her regardless.

I was wrong; the place was amazing. Besides the great location, it had two selling points for me: huge walk-in closets and in-unit laundry. Plus, it also had huge selling points for my girlfriend: a small private patio, and many people who had dogs. It also had a rooftop with views of the lake, and a diverse community—huge selling points for the both of us.

We put in an offer, and two weeks later we closed on that place.

In hindsight, I wished we had planned it better and hadn't decided to move in the beginning of

February, during a snowstorm, in the middle of a Chicago polar vortex.

Somehow, mostly thanks to the help of good friends, we managed to move to our new place. But with all the work that comes with moving, we hadn't noticed that the lock for the door that connected our new bedroom to the little patio just outside of it was broken.

We had moved the bed early in the day in the hopes that we could rest after our labors, but when we finally moved the last boxes and were getting ready for bed, our bedroom was freezing cold.

My girlfriend was on the verge of tears, but she was also too exhausted from the move to cry. She unpacked all of our blankets and threw them in the middle of the living room. She used a couple of them as a mattress and used the rest of them to cover herself and try to get warm.

Her dog cuddled up on his dog bed close to her.

The cat sat on top of one of the radiator heaters, also trying to get warm.

With boxes laying all over the place, I started to look for a sweater. That's how I found the heating blanket that I had purchased many months prior.

I plugged it in, set it to maximum, and covered myself and my girlfriend with it.

RADIATORS

I loved our new place.

But there was one thing I didn't like about it.

The radiators.

Not that I wanted central cooling and heating. Once I fixed the bedroom door, the radiators kept our new place warm; I just didn't like the way the mass of pipes that formed the radiator looked.

"We should put fancy radiator covers on them," I told my girlfriend one day.

"There is nothing wrong with them; the cat loves them," she said, pointing at her cat, who had claimed a spot on top of the radiator.

"But the place would look so much better," I started to say.

But she cut me off. "Listen, if you want to spend money that we don't have on radiator covers that we don't need, go ahead."

I knew that she was basically telling me NOT to buy radiator covers, but I only heard the go-ahead part.

The next day I called a company for a free estimate. They estimated that the covers were going to cost a couple thousand dollars. I am cheap, and that was way more than I wanted to spend.

I thought about building my own radiator covers. I even looked up the instructions on the internet. But with no proper tools or free time, it was not possible.

So, I looked on Craigslist and I found a couple of cheap covers for sale—one in Indiana, the other in Wisconsin. That was way further that I was willing to go.

A few days later while my girlfriend went to her yoga class, I went to the grocery store. On my way there I happened upon a neighborhood garage sale. I love garage sales, so I parked my car and started walking around.

To my surprise, someone was selling a group of metal radiators covers for only $25 each. Never mind the fact that I had no idea what the actual measurement of my radiators were, and therefore I had no idea if these covers would fit—I wanted them! So when the seller offered to help me bring the covers to my house, I immediately bought them.

Once I got the covers home, I realized that only one of them fit. The others could fit, but I would need to make some adjustments. I had to cut the back of one of them; two of them had the holes for the water pipes on the wrong side, so I had to cut holes on the other side before I could use them. And then there was one cover that was too tall, but if I cut it in half, I could use it to cover two of my radiators.

I fished my electrical one-inch handheld circular saw from my tool box and started to work on cutting the radiator covers.

"What the hell is all this mess?" my girlfriend asked a couple of hours later, when she came into our apartment.

I was in the kitchen with my one-inch circular saw (*pew-pew-pew*) trying to cut a metal radiator cover that I had placed on top of the kitchen counter. In the living room, there were the other metal radiator covers, along with the rest of my tools spread all over the floor.

Her dog and cat were in a corner of the room. Hiding from the noise of my saw and the mess I had made.

I tried to explain my idea to her, but she complained about the mess.

"How long is this project of yours going to take?" she asked, looking angrily at me.

I thought about that for a moment. I was trying to cut one radiator in half, cut the back of another, and make holes in the other two. In total, about a hundred inches of metal needed to be cut. So far, with my handheld one-inch circular blade saw I had been able to cut about one inch of material, and a bit of skin from my finger, in about one hour. So, if I continued to work on that project every day after work it might take five months. Maybe four months if I worked on the weekends too...

"You know I have people coming over later tonight. I hope you will be done by then," my girl said before I could respond.

"Oh, I will have it done for sure," I lied.

"I just don't understand..." *BRRRRRR* "...why you would start this project..." *BRRRRRR* "...when you know that." *BRRRRRR*

It seemed that someone was doing some kind of work right outside our window. The noise was interrupting her words, and the dog had started to bark at the workers outside.

"What is that noise?" I asked her.

"You are just trying to ignore me," my girlfriend said as another *BRRRRRRR* came from outside.

"I'm going to see what the noise is all about," I told her as I went outside to investigate. I was still holding my one-inch circular saw.

There was a construction crew repairing the outside façade of our building. These guys had tools, real tools. One guy was cutting a big chunk of cement with an unbreakable twenty-inch circular saw. *BRRRRRRR*. He cut through the cement like scissors to paper. *BRRRRRR*. His saw kept cutting; *pew-pew-pew* my one-inch saw went as I accidentally pressed the start button. *BRRRRR*. His saw kept cutting.

I hid my tiny saw behind my back, ashamed of my equipment.

Suddenly, I had an idea.

"Excuse, excuse me. Could I borrow your saw to cut something in my house?" I asked the guy holding the saw. He looked at me, at my tiny saw and my bloody finger.

"No," he said, giving me a strange look.

I explained the problem I was having with the radiators. The guy shrugged his shoulders. I explained how mad I had made my girlfriend and that I needed his help to keep me from sleeping in the doghouse for the rest of my life.

The guy looked at me for a moment. Then he replied with a heavy Polish accent, "I'll cut them if you bring them out here."

I suddenly loved all Polish people.

I ran into the building and went into my apartment. My girl was taking a shower.

I measured all the radiators, marked all the cuts that needed to be done, and brought the radiators outside, one by one, to be cut. Instead of the five months it was going to take me with the small saw, with the twenty-inch saw the whole operation took about ten minutes.

I gave the guy with the saw twenty bucks. I took the radiators back inside. I put plastic tape to the sides of the radiators that had been cut to keep them from scratching the floors. I swept around the radiators, then I put the covers over them. I put the broom aside, washed my hands, and then I sat on the sofa to contemplate my work.

"I told you I would be done before your guests come this afternoon," I told my girl just as she came out of the shower.

"Wow," she said. "Now if only you could do the same about the broken door handle, and the leaky shower, and the burnt-out light bulbs and the..." *BRRRRRRRR* the saw started going outside.

I sat on the sofa and contemplated our new—now truly perfect—place.

ONE + ONE = FOUR

I was happy with the new place.

I thought that I could turn the extra bedroom into an office for me, where the dog and cat would not be allowed and I could be free of their hair.

My girlfriend was also happy with the new place. She felt that now that we had more space, we could get a second dog.

"No way," I said when I heard her idea. "We are not getting a second dog; there's already too much dog and cat hair in this house."

A few weeks after we moved in, I was checking on the internet for a sofa for our new place. I started to look at one thing and then I ended up looking at another thing, and then another that had nothing to do with my original search.

That's how I found myself looking at pictures of dogs up for adoption.

I made the mistake of letting my girlfriend see what I was looking at. Next thing I knew, she spent the next couple of weeks browsing at pictures of dogs, and one female pit bull in particular caught her eyes.

My girlfriend asked me if we could at least have the female dog brought over to see if she would get along with her dog.

My first reaction was to be 100% against her idea, but then I thought: "Her dog doesn't like any other dog, so if we bring the female dog, her dog is going to attack it. After that happens, there's no way they will let the female dog stay here; that way, we won't get a second dog. Plus, after her dog attacks the new dog, they might take her dog away for being dangerous. I could get rid of both dogs at once."

It was worth the try.

"Go ahead," I told my girlfriend, sure that my plan was going to work.

The next day they brought the female dog to visit our house. As soon as she walked in, she curled up on the sofa.

"She is the perfect cuddle dog," the lady from the dog rescue told my girlfriend.

"I can see that," my girlfriend responded.

I wasn't happy about that. I tried to remind my girlfriend, "Honey, we don't let the dogs on the furniture."

"How about we let them meet each other?" the lady said, probably wanting to get the dogs away from me as fast as she could.

My girlfriend kept her dog leashed, explaining, "He is not always friendly to other dogs."

I looked at my girlfriend's dog, expecting it to attack the new dog.

"Get it, get it," I told the dog in my mind.

Her dog got close to the new dog. He looked at her, he smelled her, he lunged at her and then...

The two dogs started playing as if they were old friends.

Plus, the new dog didn't seem to care that we had a cat. She neither played with it nor tried to attack it.

So now, we had two dogs.

The first night the new dog stayed with us we crated her; we were trying to sleep, but the new dog was barking up a storm.

"Your dog is crying," I told my girlfriend. It was almost midnight and the next day I had to be up at five in the morning to go to work.

"Just ignore her," she replied.

An hour later the new dog was still barking. "Get your dog," I told my girlfriend.

"She will fall asleep soon," she said.

One hour later the new dog was still crying, and my girlfriend was now snoring.

I was so mad, I got up from bed. I was thinking about feeding the new the dog some chocolate, or maybe some grapes. Maybe I could open her crate, and the door to the apartment...

I walked up to her crate.

"Listen, you!" I started to scream.

But then I saw her. She looked so sad and scared. It reminded me of the difficult time I had when I was a new immigrant in this country, not knowing the language, so far from home—how I felt sad and afraid.

"OK," I said to the new dog. "I know you are scared, but we have to sleep. I have to go to work in a few hours. I tell you what, I will sing you a song so you can feel better."

I started to sing. "Go to sleep little doggy, go to sleep..."

Within minutes, the new doggy fell asleep to my song.

After that day, whenever my girlfriend gave the new dog a command like "sit" or "stay," the new dog ignored her, but if I gave her the command, she would listen to me right away. Whenever my girlfriend took the new dog out for a walk, the new dog would walk around her legs like a little helicopter, tangling her up in the leash. But if I took the leash, she walked next to me in a straight line, her tail moving at one hundred miles per hour.

The new dog became my dog.

I had to admit she was a precious little thing. She loved meeting people on the street when we took her out on walks, her tail moving nonstop as if to show how happy she was to meet them. I felt kind of proud when people commented on how cute she was.

She even helped my girlfriend's old dog to become friendlier with other dogs.

But I did notice that whenever it rained, our new dog would run around the house and hide, either under the bed or in the corner of my closet. Obviously, she was afraid of the rain.

One afternoon I was at home watching a movie with my girlfriend when suddenly it started to rain really hard. Then we started to hear one thunder clap after another.

My dog started to run around the house, looking for a place to hide.

She came into the room and jumped on the sofa between my girlfriend and me.

My girlfriend looked at me, sure that I was going to kick my dog off from the sofa.

"It's OK," I told my girlfriend. "She is afraid of the rain."

A few seconds later, her dog came into the room.

He looked at me, at my girlfriend, and my dog sitting between us, and then looked at me as if to ask:

"I thought we were not allowed on the sofa?"

So I motioned to him that it was OK to join us.

He jumped on the sofa between my dog and my girlfriend.

And it was then, as I cuddled on the sofa with my girlfriend and our two dogs, under the vigilant eye of our cat watching from her spot on the windowsill, that I suddenly realized, there was a lot of hair on the sofa, but there was even more love on it.

I was no longer afraid of dogs. And most importantly, I was deeply in love with my family.

THE LIFE OF THE PARTY

I was coming back from work when I found my girlfriend outside the house on her way back from walking the dogs. She looked at me with a scared look in her eyes.

"I cannot do this." Her dog was trying to pull away while my dog walked in circles around her, tangling the leash around her legs.

"What do you mean?" I asked, oblivious to the fact that she was having a hard time walking both of them at the same time. Until then, she had either taken them out one at a time, or I had helped taking them outside.

I took the leash of my dog in my hands; she stopped walking in circles and stood next to me. Once I took care of my dog, my girlfriend managed to control her dog.

She looked at my dog peacefully sitting next to me. "We need to take her to school."

My girlfriend works as a teacher; I thought she wanted to take my dog with her to work.

"No," my girlfriend replied when I asked if that was what she meant. "We need to take her to obedience school."

I was born and raised in a "third-world country;" my family was very poor. My parents had to struggle to afford to send my siblings and I to school. Sending a dog to school would have been out of the question.

I could almost feel the disapproving look of my ancestors.

I asked my girlfriend to let me think about the obedience school for a couple of days.

The next day, we decided to take a field trip with the dogs.

Getting them into the car was no problem at all. In fact, they seemed eager to get out of the house.

We drove a short distance and parked our car near the river walk. Each of us took our dog; we crossed the street and calmly entered the park.

Suddenly, my dog saw a squirrel and she pulled away from me, running at full speed after that squirrel, and then another. I called her, but she refused, or could not hear me.

It took a long time before I could get close enough to grab her leash. I could barely control her, and we had to cut our visit to the park short.

Once in the car, I told my girlfriend "Maybe we should take my dog to obedience school."

A few days later, we were taking my dog to school for the first time.

On our way there, my dog walked calmy next to me. But once we got close and she could hear the other dogs, she started acting worse than she had at the park when she ran after the squirrels. She panted, she whined, she barked, and she acted as if she had been waiting for this moment her whole life—and now that it was here, she couldn't wait a minute longer to get the party started.

She was like an overhyped cheerleader at a military academy. While all the other dogs stood at attention, she ran to them as if trying to introduce herself, too eager to make new friends.

"I'm sorry, I'm sorry," my girlfriend and I kept saying, as my dog kept interrupting the class by walking too close to other dogs, or whining loudly when I tried to restrain her.

It was a miracle that we didn't get thrown out that day. The following week it was more of the same. As soon as my dog could see that we were heading to the school, she would get too excited and start to almost drag me along.

I never saw anyone so happy to go to school.

She was a happy student; she just couldn't pay that much attention to the lessons. She just wanted to be part of the class; she probably felt that she was the life of the party.

And every week, on our way back home, my dog would turn back to her chill self. Walking calmy next to me, nonchalantly moving her tail as I kept asking myself: Why couldn't she act that way at school?

The day of the graduation, each of her classmates sat next to their dog parent, posing for a picture. My girlfriend and I had to carry and hold my pit bull to keep her from trying to play with the person taking the picture.

WEDDING DAY

The year prior, I had gotten tickets for a New Year's celebration, and although the end of the year was still weeks ahead, I decided to check on the one suit I had been keeping in my closet for a very special occasion. I don't know why, but my clothes seemed to shirk a little after a while, especially around the waist area. I needed to make sure I didn't have any problems with my suit when New Year's came around; after all, it was going to be a special occasion.

The shirt, the pants, and the tie from the suit were still on the hanger, but the jacket was on a separate hanger next to them. I remembered when my girlfriend's male cat had gotten sick, and how days prior to him dying, I had found him lying on the floor of the closet on top of what I thought was a piece of cloth, and that I realized later, had been my jacket.

At that time, I didn't pay attention to my jacket. I was more worried about how my girlfriend was going to react, seeing her cat so sick. But now that I looked at it, I realized that the cat had run his claws all over the collar of the jacket.

"Look at what your cat did to my jacket!" I told my girlfriend. The collar had been ripped to pieces.

She looked at me sadly...not because of my jacket, but because of her cat, who had died some years prior.

I thought: If that cat hadn't died already, I would kill it right now.

"Don't you have another suit?" my girlfriend asked, knowing that I did have at least one more.

"I have been saving that suit for a special occasion," I responded. "Maybe I can fix this one." I walked out of the room and grabbed the sewing machine.

I am short, and in the past, every time I bought a pair of pants, I ended up paying more to have them adjust them to my height than what I paid for the pants themselves. Therefore, I had taught myself to sew, to be able to fix my own clothes. But as I looked at the jacket, I realized that this was way beyond my expertise.

"Maybe they can fix it at the cleaners," my girlfriend said as she saw my frustration.

I took the jacket to a nearby cleaner, but they said that there was nothing they could do to fix it. I took the jacket to another cleaner and they offered to sell me a different jacket instead. After trying several cleaners, I finally found someone willing to help.

"I could cut a piece of fabric from the inside of the jacket, patch up the inside with a different fabric and use the fabric I took from the inside to form a new collar; that way, as long as they don't see the inside of the jacket, no one would be able to see the damage."

A few days later, I went back to the cleaners and brought the jacket back home so I could try on the whole suit.

"What do you think"? I asked my girlfriend.

She smiled and said, "It's perfect."

I looked back at her and I realized that she liked what she saw, but she wasn't looking only at the suit. She was looking past the suit; she was looking at me. She was looking past all my obvious and hidden imperfections; she was looking at the man I was starting to become, and she liked what she saw.

A few weeks later my girlfriend and I went to the New Year's celebration. She looked beautiful; I looked OK. A few minutes before midnight I interrupted the celebration. I called my girlfriend to my side, got down on one knee and asked her to marry me. To my surprise and relief, she said yes.

The very next morning, as soon as she woke up, my girlfriend asked when we were going to get married. "I don't know," I responded. "I thought my job was just asking if you wanted to get married."

"You haven't made any plans?" she asked, obviously annoyed at me.

"Well," I responded, "Would you consider having our dogs take part in the ceremony? Imagine how cute they would look, your dog wearing a tuxedo tie and mine wearing a veil."

"They are not the ones getting married," she reminded me. "Plus," she added, "imagine how crazy your dog would get around so many people; it would be worse than when we took her to school."

I had thought that our dogs could be our ring bearers, as we promised to love one another, but then I remember my dog panting, barking, and going crazy on her way to school. I imagined my dog in the middle of the wedding reception, too excited to control herself, running and bumping into people like a little Tasmanian devil. I could also see her knocking down the table holding the wedding cake, and then the cake falling to the ground almost in slow motion, and both of our dogs rushing to eat whatever was left of it.

My bride was right; it was not a good idea. In fact, that was my last input regarding our wedding. She ended up taking over the planning and execution of the wedding.

The day of our wedding, my wife—always true to herself—ended up wearing a wedding dress that her sister had used many years prior. She added a veil from her grandmother, and the wedding rings her grandparents had used. Just like when I first met her, her family and their heirlooms were still a constant presence.

For my part, I had been so worried about having a good suit for New Year's, because I had been thinking about proposing to my girlfriend that day and I wanted to make sure I looked good when I did.

When I met her, I had already been divorced twice. I was down on my luck, I was broken both financially and spiritually, and probably mentally too. I had been ripped to pieces; I was damaged. I had tried to fix myself with parties, drugs, and alcohol, and that, of course, had not worked. I had been in so many unmeaningful relationships that it felt as if no one wanted or could fix me. And that's when I met her. She was able to help me find the way to fix myself; she took a chance on me, even if I was all patched up inside.

And that's why in the end, I didn't use the suit that the cat ripped apart that day that I proposed to her. That suit, the one that was later fixed at the cleaners, looks brand new but is really all patched up inside (like me). That suit I saved for our wedding day.

Wearing that suit also made me realize that cats are special animals. After all, I had wanted our dogs to be part of our wedding but then decided against it. But somehow our cat, who had died years prior, had managed to be part of the event, in the special feline kind of way.

SPEAK ENGLISH

I was now sharing my meals, not only with my wife's dog but also with my dog. But while her dog had been often a very picky eater who accepted any piece of meat and refused to eat vegetables or fruit, my dog made no such distinctions and ate anything that I offered her.

She even ate things she wasn't offered, or even supposed to eat. She liked getting into the cat's litter box and eating the things the cat had dropped there.

We soon learned to hide the litter box.

One hot summer day, my wife was trying to cool off by eating a popsicle. My dog approached her and started barking at her, basically demanding to be given a piece of the popsicle. There was only a tiny piece left; my wife put the popsicle close to my dog's mouth expecting her to lick the remaining ice off the wooden stick. Instead, my dog opened her mouth and in one quick move swallowed both the ice and the wooden stick.

Days later, something similar happened as I ate a mango. That time it was I who, expecting my dog to just lick the bit of mango left on the pit, offered it to her and was surprised as she readily swallowed it all.

Afraid that she could get sick, we took her to the vet.

"She seems to be OK," the vet said after checking her over. "Just watch her stool to make sure she digests what she ate, and be careful when and how you feed her."

It took days for my dog to poop the remains of the popsicle stick and mango pit.

After that, we made sure to be a lot more careful whenever we fed her. Still, whenever we walked her around the neighborhood, she would quickly devour any of the many food items that people threw on the sidewalks.

One day as I walked my dogs around the neighborhood, my dog tried to eat a piece of pizza that had been discarded and was now full of ants.

"*Estas loca*, are you crazy? *Te vas a enfermar*, you'll get sick," I told her as I pulled back on her leash.

I am bilingual; my dogs are also going to be bilingual.

My wife's dog, who at times is not too friendly, took advantage of the situation and lunged for the pizza, getting dangerously close to a lady that was walking by.

"*Tu tambien*, you too?" I told him as I pulled him back.

"I don't mind if he gets close," the lady told me, looking at me and my dogs.

"He is not always friendly," I replied.

"Maybe he would be friendlier if you didn't scream at them," she said, looking at me sideways.

I tried to explain that I wasn't screaming at them, that I was simply talking to them in Spanish and that was probably why she felt my words were too loud.

"This is America," she responded. "You should speak English."

I felt attacked, so I responded.

"Yes, this is America. *Tengo la libertad de hablar cualquier idioma que yo quiera.* I have the freedom to speak any language I want."

She looked at me and barked, "Ummmmm."

Me and my dogs barked louder.

After that, we both went our own ways.

I went home, and the next morning I went to work.

When I came back from work my wife was looking at a neighborhood website that she had recently become a member of.

"Look," she said. "I think you are trending on *EveryBlock.*"

"Am I famous?" I asked her.

"Yes, but not in a good way."

I began to read the post.

Beware, there's a Mexican guy... "Wait. I am not Mexican," I said.

"Keep reading," she told me.

About five-and-a-half feet... "I wish."

Good looking... "OK, that's me."

Walking around the neighborhood, mistreating two beautiful pit bulls...

I screamed, "What the hell?"

Another comment read: *I saw him yesterday. Those people train pit bulls as fight dogs.*

Someone should call the Humane Society, another suggested.

Someone should call ICE, somebody else added.

Get those dogs away from the guy, someone had typed.

There were about twenty comments on the thread by now, some worse than others.

"I already posted a comment explaining the situation; they just ignored it. I don't understand," my wife said.

"I will make them understand," I said as I started typing a not-too-friendly comment.

My wife put her hand on my arm. I stopped typing immediately.

She wasn't talking, but I could hear her voice: Be smart, be calm, be cool.

When we first started dating, we went salsa dancing very often. One night, I was driving us back to her place in my old car. I had stopped at a gas station and had brought us a couple of sodas. I was taking a sip from my can when I drove by a parked police car.

I caught a glimpse of the police officer inside the car.

"Oh no," I said, a bit too loud.

"What happened?" My then-girlfriend asked, surprised to see me suddenly upset.

"I am about to get pulled over."

"How do you know?"

"I was drinking from the can, and the police probably thought I was drinking beer instead of soda."

"I don't think you are going to get..."

The siren, plus the red and blue lights of the police car behind us, cut off her sentence.

I pulled over, one hand grabbing the steering wheel, the other one over it, still holding my soda.

"Have you been drinking tonight?" the police officer asked when he approached my car.

"Only this," I said, tilting the can in my hand. He looked at it for a second. Then he asked, "Where are you coming from?"

"Salsa dancing," I responded. "A couple of blocks down the street..."

"And where are you heading?"

"Home."

"Anyone else in the car?"

"Just the two of us."

"Do you speak English?"

His last question surprised me as much as it upset me. I had been responding to his questions; it was obvious that I spoke English. I wanted to say, "No, I don't speak English; in fact, we have been speaking German all this time."

I was clearly upset, so much that my girlfriend had noticed.

She grabbed my arm before I could reply to the officer's question.

She was almost whispering to me, "Be smart, be calm, be cool."

"What was that?" the police officer asked.

I took a deep breath before I replied, "Yes sir, I do speak English."

He asked for my license and registration. I excused myself to fish them out of my pocket and the car's glove compartment and handed them to him.

He went back to his patrol car to check my info on his computer.

"One of your headlights is out. Make sure to get that fixed," he said, before giving me my ID back.

My now-wife still thinks that the broken light was the reason I was pulled over that night; I still believe that the officer made the assumption that I was drinking a beer. Whatever the reason, I know that she was right to tell me: "Be smart, be calm, be cool."

I might have made things worse otherwise.

And I knew, as soon as she grabbed my arm while I looked at the computer, that she meant for me to take the high road once again.

I wrote a new post with a picture of me with my dogs. I included my phone number, the number of our veterinarian, and the place from where we had rescued the female pit bull. I also added a summary of the ugly exchange I had the previous day.

I added a link on my new post to the original post that accused me of mistreating my dog.

A few minutes later the comments in the original blog started to change their tone. Then, some of them got deleted.

If you look on the website nowadays, you won't find the original post accusing me of mistreating the dogs.

It got deleted soon after.

But you might still find my post, defending me and my girlfriend.

I left it there, just in case someone else dares to accuse me again.

Because you see, people like me, people of color, we are often guilty until proven innocent.

RAIN

"Come on you two, let's go out for a walk," my wife told me and my dog as we sat lazily in the sofa watching TV. My wife loves to take long walks with her dog; me and my dog prefer short walks, and to chill on the sofa while watching TV.

I looked at my dog and she looked back at me.

"Nah, we are fine here," I responded, without bothering to get up.

My wife looked at me again. "Come on, it's a beautiful day outside."

I looked out the window and she was right. It was beautiful day. The sun was shining, the birds were singing. I looked at my dog. She was like, "Nah, I am fine here."

"Come on," I said, picking my dog up out of the sofa. My dog wasn't happy; she doesn't like to be carried. She started kicking and trying to get free. I put her on the floor, put her leash on, and started pulling her out the door.

Reluctantly, she followed me.

As soon as we got outside, she went to the patch of grass in front of the house. She did her business and started walking back inside. I understand her; like me, she doesn't like to walk, especially if it is a cold day in winter or if it is raining.

Just one more reason why she is my dog.

But today is a beautiful day, so I start to pull on her leash, forcing her to walk. We make it to the end of the block. I can see my wife and her dog already halfway to the next block. I continue to walk, trying to catch up to them, and my dog starts to turn back home again.

"Come on, it's a beautiful day," I tell her. I am dragging her. We walk five blocks before we catch up to my wife and her dog. Just then, I feel a drop of water on my skin. I look up: the sun is still there, there are no clouds in the sky.

"It's not going to rain," my wife says. My dog disagrees, again trying to walk back home.

We walk one more block before Chicago weather happens. Seemingly out of nowhere, lots of grey clouds are now covering the sun. One minute it is sunny and nice, the next minute it is raining and cold.

We are getting drenched.

We take cover under a canopy.

My dog is looking at me as if trying to say, "I told you."

The rain slows down a bit, so my wife and her dog start walking back home. I pull on my dog's leash, but she refuses to move.

I tell my dog, "Come on, let's walk before it starts raining hard again."

She refuses to move.

I pick her up. She doesn't like it. She kicks and wiggles, trying to get away.

The rain starts again; we are getting drenched again.

Still kicking and wiggling, my dog looks up at me. She is mad.

My wife and her dog are skipping in the rain, and I am trying to run and carry my angry dog.

My wife and her dog are already inside getting dry by the time my dog and I get home.

We are completely wet. I put my dog down and she starts to shake the water off her body, splashing it all over me.

"Great, I smell like wet dog," I tell my wife, who is approaching me carrying a towel.

"Poor baby," she says.

I extend my arm to grab the towel, but my wife keeps walking past me and uses it to dry my dog.

PUDDLES

After my wife left me waiting for a towel, I decided to get one of my own.

On my way to the bathroom, I stepped into a puddle right in the middle of the living room. Thinking that it was excess water from the dripping wet dogs, I grabbed a couple of paper towels and started to clean it up.

That's when the unmistakable smell of pee hit my nose.

"That's strange, we just came back from outside. They both went to the bathroom before the rain got too strong," my wife said when I notified her of my find.

I also thought it was strange, and I figured it had been a strange accident and paid no more attention to it. But to my dismay, stepping into puddles of pee became a recurring event over the next couple of days.

We started taking the dogs out more often than before, but the accidents continued. And then the female cat started behaving in strange ways. She often spent most of her time during summer on the windowsill, or on top of the radiator during the cold days, and she often slept there. But suddenly she started to go to sleep in places she had never slept before. Several times we found her inside the bathtub, under the sofa, even under our bed.

And every time we found her there, we found those places were also wet.

That's when it hit us. It was the cat, not the dogs that had been peeing all over the place.

"She never did that before," my wife noted when we realized what was going on.

My wife sat on the couch, and placing her cat on her lap, began to slowly pet her. "I think she is sick," my wife said, while her cat purred softly.

A visit to the veterinarian a couple of hours later confirmed her suspicion. Not only had she been the one peeing all over the place the last couple of days, these were also her last couple of days.

We said goodbye to her a few days later, and we donated to a nearby animal shelter the few items that she owned: her cat carriage, a few toys, and the cans of food she would no longer need.

EVERYTHING IS ALL RIGHT

"There has to be something that we can all do together," my wife said.

She was sitting on one side of the sofa while the dogs sat in between us, leaving almost no space for me.

"We are doing something together now," I said. "We are watching TV."

She threw her hands up in the air. "I mean, something besides watching TV."

"We eat tacos together every Friday" I said, reminding her of our new tradition of buying tacos for the four of us. It had replaced our Sunday morning breakfast tradition.

She looked at me. "I want us to do something together, besides watching TV or eating tacos."

The dogs looked at me. I think they agreed with me that there's nothing better than watching TV and eating tacos.

"I know," my wife said as she opened her laptop and started clicking away. A few minutes later she proclaimed: "I signed us up for a 5K."

I had so many questions.

Were we supposed to run in pairs, or as a group? And was I running with my dog, or hers? Or maybe it was a relay race? And what were we going to use as a baton? A bone, or some sort of rope? And how were we going to keep it from turning into an all-out tug of war?

It turned out that the event was not a race at all. It was more of a long walk with your dog. A 5K-long walk. And it was not a competition either, but a fundraising for one for the city's biggest animal shelters. Knowing that both of our dogs were rescues, I was glad that my wife had taken the initiative to sign us up for that event.

But I was a little bit concerned.

After all, my dog acted as if she was the life of the party, but also had a Jekyll-and-Hyde complex that could turn her into an overfriendly Tasmanian devil when surrounded by too many dogs. And my wife's dog had a history of being extremely protective and antisocial.

Even more, the event was going to take place along the lakefront, a place with more squirrels than anywhere else in the city. The presence of just one of those rodents would excite beyond control not only our dogs, but all of the hundreds of dogs that were expected to take part on the event. And there was always the possibility of rain, in which case my dog might run into hiding and refuse to come out at all.

Like I said, I was a bit concerned.

"Still says no rain," my wife told me the night before the event, as I asked for the hundredth time to check the weather report.

The next day I woke up to the sound of rain.

"It's only a small drizzle" my wife assured me as we started to get ready.

I looked at my dog and she moved her tail as if trying to assure me everything would be OK.

I still expected the worst.

To my surprise, everything worked out just fine. The rain stopped, my dog remained calm, my wife's dog didn't get into any fights. We walked the three miles without our dog, or any other dog, going too crazy over the squirrels that came out to watch the event. It was almost as if the squirrels were enthusiastic supporters at a regular run, beaming with pride and waving as their friends ran by.

Everything went smoothly; we even took a family picture with our dogs at the 5K.

On our way back home, our dogs rode in the back of my car. They had gotten plenty of exercise and even more treats from the many vendors that sponsored the event. Now they were sleeping, and cuddled up side by side.

I knew then that we could do many things together as a family.

During the following years, we took vacations to a cabin in the middle of the woods. We also went hiking with our dogs and visited numerous dog parks.

We even started taking them to the dog beach. We were no longer worried that my wife's dog would get into a fight, since my dog had made him much friendlier. And my dog had started to calm down and didn't get too excited at meeting other dogs.

At first, my wife had kept her dog leashed at the dog beach. But after a few minutes without an incident, she decided to let him run with other dogs. He had taken off and in only a few seconds had made it to the opposite far end of the dog beach.

She tried calling out his name, to no avail.

I glanced into the distance, to where he was playfully running after a dog; I called out his name.

He stopped running. His ears perked up and he looked around. Then he started running back to where I was standing with my dog by my side.

He was listening to me. I had become the leader of our pack; he had become my pal.

A couple of days later I became sure of that, not because of the fact that he listened to me, but because he also took care of me.

I was laying on the sofa, sick with a cold. I was shivering in spite of the many blankets—including the heating blanket—I was using to try to keep me warm.

"Here. This will make you feel better." My wife was giving me a bowl of chicken soup. Our dogs came into the room, knowing that even with a cold I was going to share my meal with them. As soon as we finished the soup, my dog walked out of the room. My wife's dog stood near me as I once again buried myself under the blankets.

But I was still too cold.

Moments later, my wife's dog jumped on the sofa, basically on top of me.

I wanted to tell him to go away, but I was too sick to protest. It was only after I started to finally get warm that I realized her dog was trying to make feel better.

I LOVE U 2

It was New Year's Eve, but instead of going out to celebrate with friends, we decided to watch the fireworks on TV and let our dogs sleep in our bed as a big happy family.

It was a great way to start the New Year.

But only a few days into the new year, we started to notice that my wife's dog didn't want to eat; he was having trouble walking and didn't look right. He had always been full of energy, but now he was always tired.

By now, I had learned that there are very few things in life better than coming home and being greeted enthusiastically by your dogs. But now when I was coming back from work, only my dog came to the door. My wife's dog would just look at me from where he was laying on the floor.

"What's going on?" I asked my wife.

"He must have eaten something that made him sick," my wife responded. "He should be OK soon."

But in the next couple of days his condition worsened. Until one day when he wouldn't or couldn't get up anymore.

I came back from work to find my wife sitting next to him on the floor.

I helped carry her dog out to the car.

"He is going to be OK," I told my wife as we walked into the vet's office.

After looking at her dog, the doctor came back to talk to us.

"There's a problem with his liver; with an operation he might have a few more months, but he will be in pain and there's a chance he will not survive the operation." She left to give us a few minutes to think about our options.

My wife started crying, and I reminded myself to be strong.

"I don't want to see him suffer," she said in between sobs.

We explained our decision to the doctor, and she went to get the dog so we could say goodbye.

As I saw the dog coming into the room, I couldn't believe this was the same dog I used to be terrified of. Now, I was terrified of the fact that I was not going to see him anymore.

You see, when I was a kid, before I was bitten, I actually *had* a dog. But one day he got sick, and he passed away a few hours later. It had been such a sudden and heavy loss that after that day, I had kept myself from ever having any pets.

I wasn't just afraid of dogs; I was afraid of loving another dog.

My wife was petting her dog. "You know, the people I adopted him from found him alone on a road with a metal chain embedded in his neck. He was probably abused as a puppy."

"But you made sure to give him a good and loving home," I said, hugging her.

And then I realized that when I met him, he was probably just as afraid of me as I was afraid of him.

It probably took him a long time to trust me, just like it had taken me a long time to feel safe around him, but eventually we had become friends.

I had promised myself to stay strong but before I knew it, I was lying next to him and crying like a little baby. I couldn't believe that I was ever afraid of him, or that I had wanted to get rid of him. Now I wanted more than anything to have more time with him.

As the doctor injected him, I petted and hugged him. With tears in my eyes, I told him how much I loved him. He looked directly into my eyes, and before closing them for the last time, he licked my face, as if wanting to tell me that he loved me too.

MONSTER DOG

When we got home, my dog started to walk around my wife and I, looking for her friend.

"I'm sorry honey, he is gone," I said to her, but she continued searching for him.

That night, my pit bull didn't sleep on her dog bed; instead, she laid on her friend's bed, whimpering as she went to sleep.

The next couple of days she started to lose her appetite, and every time I took her outside, she would spend an extra amount of time smelling the trees and corners that were her friend's favorite spots, as if she was trying to find him there.

"Do you think she is going to be OK?" I asked my wife.

"She misses her friend," my wife replied. "Maybe we should get another dog."

I thought that it was too soon, but I also knew that my wife was missing her dog as much as my dog did.

"I know your birthday is coming soon," I told my wife. "Maybe a new dog could be your birthday present."

"That would be the best birthday present ever," she replied enthusiastically, and without losing a minute she turned on her laptop and started searching for a new dog.

"Let's get another pit bull," she said, smiling.

"A puppy?" I asked.

"No, puppies are too much work."

After a couple of days, she had found a small, young, male pit bull she liked up for adoption.

"We should bring my pit bull, to make sure they get along," I told my wife when she told me she had made an appointment at the animal shelter.

"I am sure they will get along," she replied.

"But what if they don't? The last thing you want is to get a dog, not having them get along, and then have to take him back."

She agreed, and the following day me, my wife, and my dog went to the animal shelter.

They brought the pit bull my wife had seen online. But he was not the small pit bull we had seen in the ad; this was a bundle of muscles twice the size of my dog. My dog was terrified of him; my wife and I were terrified, too.

"It's fine," said the worker from the shelter. "We have other pit bulls she might like."

They brought a second, a third, and a fourth pit bull, but none were a good match. Instead of playing with them, my pit bull hid, trembling between my legs.

"What's wrong with you?" I asked my pit bull. "You are discriminating against your own kind."

My dog looked at me (a Latino guy) and then my dog looked at my wife (a white girl) and then my dog looked back at me.

I don't know what she was trying to tell me. But I was getting tired of seeing so many dogs she didn't like.

After a few more tries, we were unable to find a pit bull that was a good match for her.

We were about to leave.

"We do have one more dog," the worker said, and she went to the back of the facility to fetch him. She came back with a seven-month-old puppy that looked like a mix of Doberman, Rottweiler, and Husky—nothing like a pit bull.

My wife and I looked at each other with a disapproving look. We wanted a pit bull. To us, the dog we were being shown looked more like a mix of a giraffe and a bear.

But when my dog met that dog in the middle of the room, they started playing with one another.

Still, my wife and I were not convinced.

"I don't want a puppy," she reminded me.

I looked at that monster dog; it didn't look like a puppy to me. To me, he was fully grown.

"He is seven months old," the lady at the shelter commented.

"Look at his big head and long legs," my wife said, pointing at the huge dog. "He looks like a puppy that's going to grow some more."

I was afraid to think that dog could get any bigger.

My wife reminded me once again, "Puppies are too much work; we would have to house-train him."

"He is already trained," the worker assured us.

"We'll go to another shelter," I responded. "Maybe we can find a pit bull we all like there."

I started to walk out of the shelter, but I noticed that for the first time in weeks my dog didn't look sad.

That made me stop and ask my wife, "What if we bring that strange-looking puppy home for a couple of days to see if they get along?"

"I thought you wanted another pit bull," she replied.

"What I want is to see you both happy."

We went back inside the shelter and filled out the necessary paperwork to bring that crazy-looking puppy home.

That night, the dogs kept playing around the house until almost midnight. I kept trying to put them to sleep, and they kept getting up to play, like a couple of kids refusing to go to sleep at a slumber party.

"You need to go to sleep," I told them as I got up for the fifth time that night.

I took the puppy by its collar and put him inside an unlocked dog crate on the other side of the room from my dog and her dog bed.

But as soon as I made it back to the bedroom, I could hear their paws on the hardwood floor as they started yet another wrestling match.

I shook my head, I rolled my eyes, I tried to go to sleep.

I should have been mad that the dogs were keeping me up, but I was too excited about the new memories our family was going to make. Most importantly, I was happy to know that the two ladies of the house were smiling again.

THE BEST

In the first few days that our new puppy was home, he proved to be a very gentle giant.

"Are you sure about that?" my wife had asked on the second day, when I had put a tortilla chip in the palm of my hand and offered it to him.

"I will be fine," I lied, my trembling hand revealing just how scared I truly was.

To my relief, he took the chip without even touching my skin.

I remembered the people at the shelter telling us, "You are taking our best dog." At the time, I thought they were just saying that so we would adopt him.

But after I told the puppy to sit, then stay, and he listened to me, I started to believe it. And then I truly believed it when, after that, I walked a few feet away from him and placed a chip on the floor. Our puppy looked at me, and only moved when I said, "OK."

I had never been able to do that with my wife's dog.

Actually, I had failed at many things with her dog.

The first time that my wife asked me to take her dog out for a walk (back when we were dating), I took him out around the block and then I went back to sleep.

By the time my wife came back from work a few hours later, her dog had pooped in the other room. She was mad, and then she got annoyed when I saw the mess and almost puked, nearly making things worse.

I had also had failures with our second dog (the one that became my dog).

I had helped pick up and clean up after her dog so many times, that by the time we had adopted that second dog, I was used to dealing with it.

For instance, one morning after we had adopted my dog, while I was getting ready to go to work, I had suddenly stepped into a puddle of pee in the middle of the dining room floor.

"We must not have heard her bark in the middle of the night," my wife responded, half-asleep, as I informed her of the "accident."

But that dog continued to have "accidents" inside the house, so my wife and I put a bell at the bottom of the door in hopes that my dog would hit it with her paw if she needed to go out. That hadn't worked at all.

It had taken us a while to learn that when my dog needed to go, she would quickly glance at us without making a sound, then run in circles a couple of times before relieving herself. Learning that, and setting a schedule in the mornings, after work and before bed, put an end to the daily "accidents" at home, but there were still incidents now and then.

So I expected "accidents" when the new puppy first arrived, especially since he was only a few months old. But to my delight, there was never one. Not only did he walk to the door when he needed to go, but he also waited for us to get ready.

The people at the shelter were right. We had indeed adopted their best dog.

Our puppy's behavior at the obedience school corroborated it even more. From day one, our puppy proved to be a star pupil. Several times, he was chosen by the teacher to show the new lesson to the rest of the class. He was the best of his class, and he was the best dog for us.

In fact, each of our dogs (and cats) were the best in their own special way. We were lucky to have each of them in our lives.

FULL CIRCLE

"We have had so many great memories in this apartment," I told my wife as I looked around our place. Boxes containing most of our belongings were scattered all around us.

"I can't believe we are moving again," my wife said.

"What I can't believe," I responded, "is that I am helping you move, again."

As I said earlier, before we had started dating we had been good friends, salsa friends.

One day after a night of salsa dancing I had been part of a group text in which she had asked me and several of my male salsa friends to help carry items from one location to another, as our salsa friend moved from her apartment in Edgewater to her new place in Logan Square.

We had all agreed to help.

A couple of weeks later, I was at home. My teenage kids from my first marriage had come home to spend time with me for the weekend. They were playing videos games while I watched them from a short distance.

Suddenly, I received a text message: *Hi, am moving today. Are you still coming over to help me?*

It was my lady friend. I had forgotten that I had promised to help her.

"I'll be right back," I told my kids, "Don't open the door to anyone." I explained to them that I had to help a friend, but I would probably be back in only a couple of hours. I figured that since most of my salsa friends were already helping out, I would just help move a few items and then excuse myself to get back to my kids.

To my surprise, I was the only one of our salsa friends that showed up to help.

My lady friend had no one to help but her aging father, one brother-in-law with a bad knee, and another brother-in-law with only a few minutes to spare.

I remember going into her apartment and picking up a loveseat completely covered in dog and cat hair.

"I don't know if I should take that chair," my lady friend said as she saw me pick it up and heft it onto my shoulder.

Coughing as I involuntarily breathed in some of the hair falling from the chair, I responded, "You should take it to the alley, and leave it there."

"I think you are right," she responded. "Too bad, my pets really love that chair."

I remember taking the chair to the alley and then taking my shirt off to shake all the pet hair out it.

After spending more than a couple of hours putting all the heavy items into the truck my lady friend had borrowed for the move, I asked where she was moving to—more explicitly, what floor was she moving to.

"A third-floor apartment," she responded.

I had moved many times before. And if I had learned anything from all my previous moves it was that there is nothing worse than carrying heavy loads up and down several flights of stairs. She was moving out of a first-floor apartment, and I had been able to help her almost on my own. But if I was going to help her move into a third-floor apartment, I was going to need some help. Since none of our salsa friends were responding to her texts for help, I was going to have to enlist my kids.

I told my lady friend to finish packing the truck with all the small items. In the meantime, I was going to go check on my kids and meet her later at her new place to help with the rest of the move.

On the way home, I kept thinking of ways to convince my kids to help.

I could give them a sermon about the importance of helping those in need. They might agree to help, just to shut me up.

I could promise them a new video game console in exchange for their help. However, extortion might be a quick solution that would prove costly in the long run.

Maybe I could just remind them that I was their father and, as my kids, I expected them to do as they were told. But as a weekend parent, I knew that this was most likely the worst course of action, and the one that could prove least effective.

"I need your help," I told my kids as soon as I got home.

My daughter and my son stopped playing the video game and looked at me.

"My friend is moving, and she has too much stuff..." I couldn't think of what else to say.

"OK," they both said as they turned off the game and started walking towards the door.

I felt so proud of them.

When we got to my lady friend's new place, I felt even prouder, as they carried many loads of not-too-heavy stuff up and down the stairs, while I helped carry most of the heavy items.

At the end of the day, my lady friend showed her gratitude by buying us a couple of pizzas, which my kids devoured gratefully.

"So, is she your girlfriend?" one of my kids, I don't remember which one, asked when I was driving them back home.

"No," I responded. "She is my friend; I like her, but I couldn't date somebody with pets."

Little did I know at the time that only a few years later I would not only be dating my lady friend, but married to her, and in love with her pets. I would even have a dog of my own. We would be living together back in Edgewater and be getting ready to move once more.

"What are you thinking about?" my wife asked, interrupting my thoughts.

"No one is helping us move this time." I thought about my kids, now far away and grown up, busy with their own lives. I thought about my aging body; now I was the one with a bad knee and an injury-prone back. And I thought about our friends, the ones that had helped us move there, now like me, also getting old.

"That's why we hired movers," my wife said, as if reading my thoughts. "It will be much easier this time."

"That, and the fact that we are not moving onto a third floor." I looked at my dog. She was getting old, and we had purposely searched for and found a first-floor apartment, since going up or down stairs was getting difficult for her.

"He will be happy with the extra space," my wife said, looking at her dog. He was now much older, but I still saw him as a puppy; many times he had run into the walls of our apartment when he found himself short of room to run.

"I think *you* will like the added space," I said to my wife. I reminded her of the time she had been on a Zoom meeting and her students had asked if she had the radio on because they had heard me signing Mexican *ranchera* songs while in the shower.

My wife shook her head at the memory.

"I am going to miss this place," I said once again, looking around.

"Me too," my wife said. I hugged and kissed her.

"Maybe we could take a piece of this place with us." I pointed to one of the radiator covers that I had found for our place.

When we had put our place on the market, I had thought that the radiator covers were going to add value to the place. However, our real estate agent had adamantly recommended that we get rid of them. Since I couldn't leave them there, I had hoped to take them with us to our new place, but the radiators there were of different sizes, and they all had custom covers already on them.

My wife gave me a look. "You know what you have to do," the look said.

I took the covers to the alley.

Five minutes later, when I went to take the garbage out, the covers were gone.

The most likely reason for their disappearance is that one of the many trucks that travels up and down the Chicago allies collecting scrap metal drove through, and one of its passengers had taken the old metal covers to be sold as scrap.

But I like to think that someone saw the radiator covers in the alley, rushed to collect them, and put them to good use in their own now-perfect apartment.

DOUBLE THE FUN

Our puppy was now a young dog. He had proven to be a magnificent addition to our family.

No one was happier to have him than my dog. They got into wrestling matches that lasted for hours.

My wife was getting concerned that they would never stop, especially since my dog was getting old and didn't seem to have enough energy to keep up with our young dog.

"We need to buy him a toy," my wife said one day as we were buying dog food at the pet store.

"How about this one?" I showed her a squeaky toy which promised hours of fun.

"He will rip that away in minutes," she said, showing me how the package ranked it as a Number 1, indicating that it was meant for much smaller dogs. "The strongest toy is ranked at Number 10."

"So what number do we need for our dog?"

"He should be OK with a Number 7."

After all our young dog hadn't tried to chew on our shoes or furniture; surely a Number 7 toy would be enough for him.

Once we got home, it took less than a minute for our young dog to destroy the stuffed animal and remove the squeaky ball that had been hidden in the middle of it.

The next week my wife bought a Number 8.

It took longer to get the toy home than our young dog took to destroy it.

The following week, we went straight for a 10, the strongest one they had. Surely that would be enough.

"This might last at least a couple of days," I said, paying for the toy.

Once home, our young dog took less than a minute to prove me wrong.

For the next couple of weeks, we tried different brands and kinds of toys, all of them advertised to last forever. Some of them did last a couple of days, but only if we were able to take them away from our young dog before he completely destroyed them.

I was getting tired of seeing our money get ripped away every time the young dog ripped apart a toy.

While trying to take one of those unfortunate stuffed animals away from him, I accidentally discovered that he enjoyed playing tug-of-war. I ran to the closet where we kept some old dog toys, and I fished out an old knotted rope.

At first, our young dog seemed excited about it. And I was excited at the prospect of not having to waste more money on stuffed toys for him. But after a short while he started trying to rip the rope to pieces.

My wife continued to buy stuffed animals, though. Our place started to look like one of those spooky places on scary movies where it is full of corpses. Except in our place, it was stuffed animals that found their early demise.

I am cheap, I didn't want to buy any more toys for our young dog.

One day my wife asked me to stop by the pet store on the way home from work and buy dog food.

While waiting in line to pay, I suddenly saw something that caught my attention. It was an unusual dog toy. It was made out of rubber instead of cloth. It was shaped like a letter S, and it was sky blue. According to the package, it was the strongest toy on the market. In spite of the previous disappointments with other ultra-strong toys, I decided to give it a try.

"Look at this blue guy," I said to my wife once I got home.

"You think he is going to like it?"

"Only one way to find out."

I showed the blue guy to our young dog, and he immediately bit into one end of the toy, and the best thing was that it didn't break or get ripped to pieces. I pulled at the other end and soon we were stuck in a tug-of-war game. I won, but I was too tired to keep playing, so I tossed the blue guy across the room. Our dog ran after it, took it into his mouth and brought it back to me. He had never fetched before.

I had found the perfect toy for him.

We started bringing the blue guy out most of the time when we took our young dog for a walk. If we brought him to the dog park or the dog beach, he would play tug-of-war with other dogs. And he always won.

The best thing about the blue guy was that it was stronger than any other toy. It took months before it started to show signs of wear and tear.

By that time taking walks by the beach during the weekends had replaced our old walks to the park. One day while we walked along the beach, he got into a tug-of-war with another dog, and this other dog did not back down.

Soon, the other dogs owners walking their dogs along the beach were getting closer to see what was going on. Meanwhile, the dogs growled and pulled at opposite ends of the blue guy, while the number of people around then got larger and larger. I suspected that most of them resented our young dog because he had beat their dogs; I was sure they wanted to see him lose.

"Did you bring your phone?" I asked my wife. I wanted to record the epic dog contest, but I had just realized that I had left my phone at home. She shook her head. I looked around to see if anyone was recording, but everyone was too busy watching the action.

Just then, both dogs pulled at the blue guy with all their might, and the toy broke in half.

"WOW," we exclaimed, as the crowd erupted in cheers. Some declared how they had expected one dog or the other to win but never expected the fight to end in a draw.

"I'm sorry, please tell me where I can buy your dog another toy." The owner of the other dog was trying to apologize that the blue guy had ended up broken in half.

I told her not to worry about it; I assured her that I had already brought another toy for my dog. But I did tell her where to buy one for her dog.

The next week, we were again walking our young dog around the lake. He was proudly carrying a brand-new toy in his mouth.

A dog owner approached me. "What an epic battle that was last week." He lamented that no one had recorded the event. "Maybe it will happen again," he said. "The other dog is right over there." He pointed at where the owner of the other dog was throwing a toy that her dog eagerly ran to fetch.

"Well, it looks like they both have a new toy," I said, pointing to the new toy our dog was holding in his mouth.

At that moment, the other dog ran to us. He was holding a toy in his mouth, but it was a toy of a different kind.

My wife and I looked at one another in surprise.

"Is that a double-headed dil..." I started to ask, but then the other dog owner approached us.

"I see your dog has a new toy," I said.

"It's not like yours" the lady said.

"No it's not. Not at all," I responded.

She shrugged. "At least I didn't have to buy it."

I was afraid to ask. In silence, I looked at my wife.

"My ex-roommate left it in my place, and my dog found it under the bed," the lady said. She started pulling at one of the heads, and her dog was biting the other head. She smiled. "Maybe the dogs will get into another epic tug-of-war."

"I don't think so," I responded before I could stop myself.

Surprised at my response, the lady glanced sideways at me.

"I wouldn't want your toy to break" I said, excusing myself and starting to walk away.

Our young dog didn't want to leave, so I told him while I pulled at his leash, "You are way too young to play with those adult kind of toys."

DEAD BODY

We had moved to Rogers Park, a very diverse part of the city of Chicago, near the lakefront. As such, we are often unwilling witnesses of BBQs, birthday parties, and the occasional wedding.

One morning as my wife and I walked with our dogs on the beach, we found a suspicious-looking package on the sand in a heavy-duty black plastic bag.

Our dogs went crazy, sniffing and trying to rip the bag open.

I got close to the bag, wondering what could be inside of it.

The dogs had made a small hole in the bag, and something that could only be described as blood was dripping from it. I tried lifting the bag, but a horrible putrid smell came out of it.

"Oh my, what's in there?" my wife said as she caught a whiff of the smell.

"I don't know," I replied. "It could be anything."

I had been watching too much TV. In my mind, I immediately thought of a dead body, perhaps a victim of drug cartels, a serial killer, or a gang dispute.

I didn't know what to do. I couldn't just leave the bag there. To my dismay, I did the only thing left to do. I turned into Becky and called the police.

My wife looked at me. "We should leave before the police get here; they might think you did it."

I was about to ask why the police would think of me as a suspect but then I remembered. I am a person of color; we are always suspects.

I started trying to remember what I had seen on TV shows. Could plastic surfaces hold finger prints? Could I erase them?

Maybe I should make sure I didn't leave behind any DNA, any hair...maybe I should erase my footprints...

But then I remembered, I had called them. They already had my phone number.

We stayed, and a few minutes later a police car arrived.

I showed the location of the bag to one police officer, while a second police officer and then a third started to approach the scene.

They told me to stay back a little.

The police officers approached the bag. One of them put a mask on, then a second mask and then a third. The officer with the masks got down on one knee and ripped the bag open.

The smell got stronger. I could hear my wife from further down the beach trying to calm the dogs as they whined and pull on their leashes.

A police officer covered his mouth, took a few steps back, turned around and started to puke. The other one got on the walkie-talkie.

"Blood...*sssshh*...head...*sssshhh*...pieces...*ssshhh*..."

I went back to tell my wife.

"I think, they found a dead body inside the bag."

I waited for the police to start putting the crime scene tape around the plastic bag. But they just got in their cars and stayed there.

I started approaching the scene. I could not help it, I wanted to see. I needed to see.

It was a dead body.

The victim had been tied up, decapitated, gutted and cut into pieces.

I was basically alone with the dead body; there was only one thing left for me to do.

I grabbed my phone and took a picture.

Then I ran back to where my wife was waiting with our dogs.

I tried showing the picture to her.

"No, I don't want to see it," she said, pushing the phone away.

"But it is a good picture," I said trying to show it to the dogs.

"How could you take a picture of that?" she asked, mad.

I thought it was a very good picture, so good that if I were to post it on Instagram, it might go viral and I could become famous.

But my wife didn't agree.

"What's the problem?" I asked "Have you never seen a dead chicken before?

"A chicken?" she replied, finally looking at the picture.

We live in a very diverse part of the city of Chicago, and since we live near the lakefront, we are often unwilling witnesses to BBQs, birthday parties, weddings, and the occasional remains of a chicken or two that had probably been killed as part of some kind of santeria or voodoo ceremony.

After my wife saw the picture, she started to walk away.

"Wait for me!" I screamed, while trying to put my phone in my pocket.

"Well, hurry up then," she said, while pulling at the leash; our dogs were still trying to get back to the garbage bag. They wanted chicken.

I took a few steps and saw half-buried on the ground what I thought was a tennis ball.

"Oh, an orange," I said as I picked the round object from the sand.

My wife looked back. There were several oranges spread around the beach.

"There were probably left over as part of the ceremony," I told my wife.

"Don't eat them," my wife responded. "It could be disrespectful."

"But they are so yummy," I responded. I had already peeled the orange and was taking bites out of it.

My wife shook her head. I suspected that she was secretly hoping she could put a leash on me, too.

ZOMBIE DOG

It was around three in the morning, and we were on our way to the hospital.

The previous night, my now-twelve-year-old pit bull had woken up in the middle of the night and started running around the house nonstop.

At first, my wife took her out to pee, but that didn't calm our dog. My wife woke me up, and I found our dog foaming at the mouth, running in circles and panting excessively.

"We have to take her to the emergency veterinarian," my wife said.

"Let me send an email to my job to let them know I'm not coming to work," I responded.

"OK, I will keep an eye on her," my wife responded, and to keep the dog from running around the house, she locked the wo of them up together in the washroom. A few minutes later I opened the door just as my dog pooped and walked in circles all over the poop.

My wife looked at me. "I'll clean her up; get the car ready."

Soon we were on our way. As I got out of the driveway, I could see our young dog looking at the window, wondering where were we taking his friend.

I started driving while my wife sat in the back with my dog, who was twitching, foaming at the mouth, and pissing and pooping all over my wife. With every passing minute, we grew more fearful that this would be my dog's last night with us.

By the time we got to the vet, my dog could no longer walk. I carried her inside and stood by the desk as my wife gave our information to one of the nurses.

"Give her to me," a doctor rushing from inside the hospital said. The doctor started running back into the hospital. She paused to ask if we gave consent to have our dog treated.

"Do whatever you need to do," my wife and I responded. The doctor turned around and carried my dog inside.

A nurse came running a few minutes later; she took us to a waiting room while they took care of my dog.

A couple of minutes later, the doctor came into the room.

"Your dog had a very high fever. We have to sedate her to bring the fever down. We placed her in a bath of ice. If the fever goes down, we can begin to treat her."

That didn't sound good at all. The only thing we could do was nod and wait for more news.

I remembered that first night my dog came to our home, when she wouldn't go to sleep and cried nonstop. I remembered how I was upset, how I got up with the intent to shut her up, and how once I saw her sad little face, I couldn't bring myself to be mad at her, and had ended up singing her a lullaby to her instead: "Go to sleep little doggy, go to sleep little doggy, go to sleep."

Now, we feared the worst. Would I have to sing to her as she went to sleep for the last time?

A couple of hours later, the doctor came back into the room.

"Your dog had a seizure and seems to have lost sight in one eye, but she is responding to the medication. We can take you inside if you want to see her."

My dog was drowsy from the medicine and could barely move, but it was great to see she was no longer as frantic as at the beginning of the night, or as comatose as when I carried her in.

We were asked if we wanted to come back the next day, or wait a couple of hours to see if she got better and we could take her home.

We decided to wait.

Around 7 AM, the doctor came into the room again. She gave us some medicine (steroids and anti-seizure pills) and we were allowed to take my dog back home.

It was a long night that only got longer when we got home and my dog refused to go to sleep.

I tried singing to her: "Go to sleep little doggy, go to sleep." But it was no use.

Earlier that night we were afraid that she would close her eyes forever; now we were hoping she would close them at least for a couple of hours so we could get some sleep.

"Please go to sleep," I kept telling my dog as she walked back and forth around the house.

My wife and I passed out in the living room while my dog kept walking nonstop.

When I woke up a couple of hours later, my dog was still walking around the house, whimpering a little bit every few minutes. She kept bumping into the walls as she walked, probably from not being able to see as well as before. It hurt to see her like that.

She kept having small seizures, which made her twitch, foam at the mouth, and growl a bit. I love my dog, but she kind of looked like a zombie dog; she made me remember a movie where a dog gets beaten by zombie dogs and then its owner has to kill his dog as it is turning into a zombie dog.

I looked at my dog and finally understood why so many people refused to kill off their infected loved ones and end up getting turned into zombies in those movies.

"Are we being selfish by forcing her to stick around?" I asked my wife, holding back tears.

Fearing that my dog was going to have a huge seizure, we decided to take her back to the vet.

But when the doctor saw my dog, she immediately told us she was doing so much better, and assured us that her frantic, zombie-like state was due to the medicine and not to an impending seizure. We were given another medicine to calm her down, and once again were blessed to take my dog back home.

That night I was glad to see that my dog was doing so much better. I sang to her, "Go to sleep little doggy, go to sleep." And we both went to sleep at a normal hour.

STUCK

While the two ladies of the house—my wife and my dog—got some much-needed rest, I took the young dog out for a walk by the lake.

By now, he had taken up a couple of new pastimes. Every time he found a ball at the beach—and there always seemed to be some kind of tennis ball, plastic ball or squeaky plastic toy left behind there—our dog would grab it in his mouth, put it in the sand, and start digging a hole in which to bury his treasure. Most times he would place the treasure he was trying to bury in the hole, only to have it flung out of the hole by his own paws as he tried to bury it.

I loved our young dog, but in those moments, I often wondered if there was any other animal quite so silly. His other pastime consisted of finding sticks in the sand and chewing them to little pieces. Sometimes he would get so concentrated on destroying a stick that he would completely forget about the ball he had been playing with, and end up losing it in the sand.

I loved walking by the lake with the dogs, too. The bad thing is that no matter how cold or how hot it might get, there was always at least one couple in their car, parked at the end of our street in the cul-de-sac that overlooks the lake.

I often saw the parked cars rocking back and forth, and I knew they were not rocking because of the wind. It was like a drive-thru motel out there.

That morning, I didn't see a car parked in the cul-de-sac. But something worse was going on.

Our young dog started growling as we entered the path from the street to the beach. He rarely growls, so I asked, "What is it?" I tried to see what he was growling at.

It took me a while to believe what I was seeing was real. There was a car on the beach!

It turned out that some kid had wanted to get himself and his girl closer to the water and managed to get stuck in the sand. A guy had stopped by and was trying to help the kid get his car out. I offered to help, too. I let go of the leash and told my dog to wait, then I joined in. We pushed the car while the girlfriend put it in reverse and hit the gas, but it was no use. The two front wheels were buried in the sand.

"We need to put something under the tires to get some traction," the guy told the kid.

I grabbed the leash and walked a few feet away to where I remembered seeing a piece of wood the day before. At first our dog got excited, thinking I had found the piece of wood for him so he could chew it to pieces. He got a bit sad when I took the wood back and we started to use our hands to dig in the sand to try to put the wood under the tires, to create a bit of traction and get the car out. But after a while, even the young dog wanted to help; he started to dig in the sand with his paws.

But even with the piece of wood, the car was going nowhere.

I excused myself to continue walking our dog. I took him out on a short walk and then took him back home.

Then I went into the basement in search of a shovel.

"I came back to help," I said to the kid as I got back to the lake. "I would hate for the police to get here before you could get the car out."

"Would they give me a ticket?" the kid asked, concerned.

"They would call a tow truck, impound your car, and give you a couple of tickets," the other guy explained.

"And you would have to take an Uber home and then go get your car back," I added.

"But honestly," the guy continued, "I am more worried about what your girlfriend is going to say to you when you get home."

"At least this will be a night she won't forget," I said, and we all started laughing.

We tried again to push the car. But it was in vain.

For a moment I contemplated the idea of getting my car, tying a rope to his car, and pulling it out. But my car was half the size of his car.

Then it would be two cars stuck, I thought.

"You are going to have to call a tow truck," we finally said to the kid.

"How much would that cost?" the kid asked.

"Whatever it is, is going to be a lot less than what the city and the police tickets will cost you."

He agreed, and we waited for the tow truck. He needed to get his car out, and I was curious to see how it was going to get done.

Ten minutes later the tow truck arrived, and its driver backed up into the beach, started to lift the car stuck in the sand, then tried to move forward, only to get stuck in the sand.

The tow truck driver got out, unhooked the car from the tow truck, and proceeded to move back and forth, back and forth for about ten minutes until it finally got free.

"I'm going to have to go get some help," the driver told the kid. "You got money to pay?"

The kid looked defeated. "Fine," he said. "I just need to get out."

The driver left and returned ten minutes later, followed by a second, much-larger tow truck. By now, the police had also arrived. The driver of the tow truck started to explain the situation to the other tow truck driver.

"Yeah, I pulled cars out of there before," he interrupted. "Here's what we need to do."

He attached one end of a long chain to his tow truck and the other end to the car stuck in the sand. It took almost twenty minutes of tugging, but the car was finally out.

The kid sped out of there; hopefully he had learned his lesson. I went back home to get our young dog and continue our walk.

In the weeks that followed, I saw many other cars stuck on the sand, but I didn't try to help push them out anymore. I now knew that only a tow truck could pull them out. And now when I saw my puppy burying his treasure in the sand, I knew that he might be a bit silly, but nowhere nearly as silly as the people who drove their car into the sand.

"You know, our young dog almost got stuck in the lake too," my wife said as we walked around the marks left by yet another car that had been towed away the day before.

"Did he try to bury a toy in the sand only to find himself in a hole to deep for him to climb out? I asked my wife; I had seen huge holes that he had easily dug before.

"Actually," my wife said, "the other day he saw a duck in the water, and before I could stop him, he ran onto the pier and then jumped into the lake and swam after the duck."

And of course, the duck had flown away as soon as our dog had swum too close. And then our puppy had swum some more, only to have the duck fly away again and again.

"He swam so far that I thought he wasn't going to be able to swim back," my wife said, "and the water was so cold I thought he was going to freeze to death, but finally he gave up and came back."

I shook my head thinking: what a silly dog. He was sitting in the sand a few feet away from us; I asked, "What is he doing now?"

"Chewing a stick," my wife responded. But then she looked at him some more.

Our dog was shaking his head, making noises as if trying to puke. He was trying to scratch his mouth with his paws. He looked like he was choking. As we got closer, we were able to see that a piece of the stick had gotten lodged sideways in his mouth. I tried to reach into his mouth and unstick the stick, but I feared that he would accidentally bite my hand. I also feared that the stick would cut his mouth if I tried to pulled it out.

My wife started to talk to him, trying to calm him down.

"I need to get some scissors," I told my wife, thinking that I could try to put them inside his mouth and cut in half the piece of stick that was stuck in his mouth.

I rushed home and, fishing a pair of pliers from my toolbox, I headed back to the beach. By now my wife had calmed our young dog enough that I was able to stick the pliers into his mouth and break the piece of wood in two and get it out of his mouth.

Our dog jumped up, drank a bit of water from the lake and then tried to go back to chewing the stick.

We put his leash back on and started to walk back home.

LESSON

It was five o'clock in the morning, and there was no one by the lake.

I was walking my dog. She was old now, so old that at times I had to carry her up and down the stairs to our place. I even got her a tiny step ladder so she could climb on the sofa, since she could no longer jump that high.

She was so old that I was not really walking her. It was too slow to count as walking. She took one slow step after the next.

My wife was walking her dog. Her dog was no longer a puppy but he was still young, so she was not really walking him. It was more like trying not to be dragged by him as he pulled and jumped, trying to get free of the leash.

"Do you want some help?" I asked my wife as she almost lost control of her dog.

She responded, "Please."

I grabbed the leash, and he immediately stopped pulling and jumping.

"How did you do that?" my wife asked, surprised.

"I have been training him. Just watch this."

I told her dog "Sit," and he sat on the sand.

My old dog also sat near the water and started licking the sand, trying to find some small fish to eat.

I took a few steps. "Come" I told her young dog, and he started to follow me. My old dog walked slowly close by.

"Sit," I told her young dog again, and as he sat, I undid his leash.

My wife was a bit nervous, but I assured her everything was OK.

"Wait" I told her dog, and he didn't move as I undid my old dog's leash. She sat down and starts licking the sand again.

I grabbed a stick, and her dog's ears lifted in anticipation.

"Wait," I said, and I threw the stick into the water. Her dog looked at me.

"Ok go get it," I said, and her dog ran into the water after the stick.

"Wow, you really have them trained," my wife said as she got close to me. Her young dog brought the stick back to me and I threw it once again into the water.

"Go get it, go get it."

He ran into the water while our other much-older dog sniffed the sand next to me.

My wife was looking at her phone; she had to head back home for a work Zoom meeting. She waved goodbye to me and the dogs and started to walk away.

When the young dog saw that she was leaving, he started running after her.

I whistled and he came back to me.

"Wait until I throw the stick!" I screamed at my wife. "He will be distracted, and then you can leave."

I threw the stick and our young dog ran back into the water; my wife ran home.

After a couple times retrieving the stick from the lake, our young dog suddenly realized that my wife had left, and he took off running after her. I whistled and screamed commands: "Wait! Stop! Come! Sit!" but he was not listening. He was still running. I started running, too.

(I don't know if you have ever tried running on the beach; it is very difficult.)

Our young dog was so fast he was already out of the beach and running onto the small patch of grass past the beach. I was afraid he would run into the road and get hit by a car.

Suddenly he stopped. He was looking at a lady who he had confused with my wife.

I willed myself to run faster, trying to catch up with him.

But now he was running again. He made a left into the park, away from the road. When I got to the edge of the park, I saw him at a distance, chasing a squirrel. After that one got away, he ran after another squirrel, and then one more.

I whistled and screamed commands: "Wait! Stop! Come! Sit!" but he had squirrel fever now.

A squirrel ran into some high bushes, followed closely by our young dog. That's when I lost sight of him.

"Maybe I should run home and get my bike, so I can cover more ground," I heard myself thinking.

"But I will lose precious time," I argued with myself in my head.

And that's when it hits me.

In my rush to catch our young dog, I left our older dog by the lake by herself. I had to make a decision: either I had to keep trying to catch our young dog, or go back for our older dog. I couldn't lose them both.

I didn't know where our young dog was, but I had an idea where I could find our old dog.

I decided to get back to the beach; after all, we could always get another puppy.

"That's not nice," I heard myself thinking.

"I'm just kidding," I told myself.

I ran onto the beach as fast as I could, screaming our old dog's name. I prayed that she hadn't followed me and gotten lost as well.

(I don't know if you have ever tried running on the beach after running around for a few minutes; it is very difficult.)

I saw her at a distance; she was still sitting by the lake, sniffing the sand away. I ran up to her and put her leash on. I tried to run back to the park to continue searching for our young dog, but she didn't want to leave, so I was basically dragging her.

(I don't know if you have ever tried running on the beach while dragging an old dog; it is almost impossible.)

We were moving so slow I knew we were never going to find our young dog.

"Is that your dog running around?" a lady asked when I finally make it back to the edge of the park. She knew I lost a dog because I had been screaming his name.

"Where is he?" I asked, and she pointed to a small spot far away.

"Why would you let him off leash?" the lady asked, mad at me.

"Not now lady," I replied. I was not mad at her, I was mad at myself.

"I need a stick," I told myself aloud as I reached a tree and broke off a small branch.

I started waving the stick in the air as I tried to get close to my runaway dog.

I tried to whistle but my mouth was dry from running around. Instead, I screamed commands: "Wait! Stop! Come! Sit!" Then I realized how contradictory and confusing those commands were.

After a few seconds, our young dog gave up trying to catch a squirrel. He saw me shaking the stick and ran back to me. He was tired, and I was able to grab him and put his leash back on.

"You are back," my wife said when we got home.

"We almost didn't make it back," I responded, and I told her how I almost lost our dogs.

"From now on," I said, "if we go out together, we come back together."

My wife nodded in agreement.

That day I tried to show off how I had been training and teaching things to our dogs, but the truth is that they are the ones that had been teaching me.

I had learned that you can indeed teach new tricks to an old dog.

They taught me to be patient, that it takes time to learn new things.

They taught me that family is not only those you are born into but also those you meet along the way.

They taught me that you are never too old to be sung a lullaby.

They taught me that humans are the silliest of animals, and dogs might be the wisest.

They taught me that you can learn to get along with and even love others, in spite of their differences.

They taught me to face my fears and overcome them.

They taught me to give love a chance.

COINCIDENCE?

Although I loved our dogs, I didn't always look forward to walking them and having to pick up their poo, especially when I just got home from work and instead of getting to relax and watch TV for a couple of minutes, I had to walk around the neighborhood freezing my ass off.

One day I was walking our dogs when I saw a lady friend of mine that I had not seen in a very long time.

"OMG, you look as young as ever!" she said to me as we met in the street.

Before I could answer her, one of our dogs took a big dump.

"Sorry, I have to get this," I said, and started picking up the shit.

I tried to continue the conversation with my friend, but it was just awkward trying to talk while holding a bag full of poo.

Soon, both of us were making excuses to end the conversation and go on our separate ways.

A few days later I was again walking the dogs, and I came across a couple of young ladies that smiled at me and the dogs as we walked down the street. As if on cue, one of the dogs took a big dump. It was a bad sight, and the smell was even worse. The ladies crossed the street without taking another look at me or the dogs.

I realized that my dogs had the surprising ability to shit whenever I met someone in the street.

Soon after that I was again walking the dogs, when I suddenly bumped into an ex-girlfriend.

It was an awkward encounter; things had not finished smoothly between us. But before I could even say hi to the ex-girlfriend, the dogs pulled at the leashes and both of them started to take a dump. However, this time it was obvious that the dogs had eaten something that had upset their stomachs.

A horrible-looking and -smelling liquid was spraying from their rear ends.

It didn't even look like they were taking a shit. In fact, it looked like they were trying to write a message in the snow. *BYE*. Or maybe it was *Go AWAY*. I really couldn't tell. Their ass-writing was hard to read and not something you wanted to get close enough to inspect.

I didn't even bother to see if the ex-girlfriend had stuck around to talk with me. I took my time cleaning up the mess the dogs had made, and then I had to find a garbage can to dispose of it.

By the time I got back home, my wife was already home, and the dogs jumped all over her.

"Be careful," I told her. "They are sick."

"Oh no, they have been so good," she said. "I have been training them, too. You want to see?" She took a couple of treats in her hand. "Give me a paw," she said, and each of the dogs put their paw in her outreached hand. "See? I trained them," she said, smiling.

I smiled back, wondering if she had also been training them to shit as soon as I met someone on the street, or if that was just a perfectly-timed coincidence.

TACOS

The doorbell to our apartment rang one day. The dogs started barking loudly.

It was a cold Friday afternoon. I rushed to the closet to put on a sweater. Then I went out to the door to pay the delivery man.

I opened the building's door, and the delivery guy started to recite my name and address to ensure I was the proper recipient.

Suddenly, he stopped talking and moving; his eyes got big as saucers.

I looked around and noticed that in my rush, I left the door to my apartment open, and my two dogs had followed me into the hallway and were now standing beside me.

"Are they going to bite me?" he asked, still unable to move.

I looked at my dogs. "No, they haven't even barked at you. They are here for the tacos."

The guy looked at me; he was a bit confused.

Every Friday, either my wife or I would stop by a neighborhood Mexican restaurant and buy a few tacos. However, every now and then life got too busy, and we ended up having the tacos delivered home. But whether we picked them up or had them delivered, we always bought a few tacos for our dogs. Lately we had been so busy that almost every Friday we'd been having the tacos delivered—so often, in fact, that when someone rang the doorbell our dogs would get mad when I came back inside and had the audacity to not bring them any tacos. They started barking and howling as if demanding to know, "Where are my tacos?"

That Friday, they must have smelled the tacos and followed me out to the door to pick them up. I knew that my dogs were not going to hurt the delivery guy, but I also knew the fear of suddenly having a dog or two in front of you.

I apologized for being careless. I tipped him generously, and he went on his way.

GO TO SLEEP LITTLE DOGGY

We had spent a wonderful afternoon together as a family eating tacos and watching TV, but that night my dog woke us in the middle of the night.

For months after getting sick, she had had tiny seizures that lasted for a couple of seconds, but this time she was having a very bad seizure. She kept walking around the house, bumping into the walls. Her friend, our other dog, was walking around the house after her, at times trying to hold her back with his paw.

It was heartbreaking to see.

"We have to take her to the hospital," I told my wife; she agreed, and minutes later we were on our way.

I could see our other dog looking through the window of the house as we drove his friend away.

My wife kept telling me, "It's going to be OK. They will give her some more medicine, just like before." But I could see the worry in her eyes.

By the time we got to the hospital, my dog was unresponsive. I carried her inside, just like the previous time, and just like before, we were told to wait in a room while the doctors took care of her.

A couple of hours later the doctor came into the room and told us: "She is calm now; we will keep an eye on her, but she seems to be responding well to the medicine."

"So, we should be able to take her back home today?" we asked.

"It appears to be that way," the doctor responded. "But, let's wait a couple of hours before we can tell for sure."

Less than an hour later, the doctor came back into the room.

"She had two more seizures," the doctor announced. "At this point there is very little that can be done."

We had the choice to keep medicating her to keep the seizures in control for a day or two, or just let her go to sleep.

I wanted to sing to her one last time.

They brought her into the room. She was sleeping, snoring a little as she often did.

We started to cry. I cuddled her, got close to her and sang into her ear.

"Go to sleep little doggy, go to sleep."

I watched as the doctor injected her.

I continued singing to her.

"Go to sleep little doggy, go to sleep."

The doctor kept talking, but I wasn't listening anymore. I just kept singing to my dog, "Go to sleep little doggy, go to sleep."

I sang to her until she stopped snoring. I hugged her, I kissed her and sang to her one last time.

I don't remember how or when, but I drove home somehow.

I was heartbroken, sure that I was never going to find another dog like her.

DEALBREAKER

A couple of weeks later, my wife started pointing at her dog laying in the middle of the living room. "He needs a friend to play with."

I also needed a new friend. I missed having my dog cuddle up with me while watching TV, or laying by my feet in bed, snoring as we slept. But I felt that it was too soon.

It took a couple more months before I started to consider getting another dog. In fact, I only agreed to look at dogs for adoption as an anniversary gift to my wife. But still, I made sure to give one condition: "It had to be another pit bull."

We spent the next couple of weeks going to shelters and meeting pit bulls. Many of them licked my face or jumped in my lap as soon as we met them.

But my wife's dog would not even look their way. I was getting frustrated; I remember thinking, "Maybe we should leave her dog here and bring two pit bulls home instead."

As if reading my mind, my wife suggested: "Maybe we should get you a dog of a different breed." I disagreed. I was determined to get another pit bull.

After weeks of searching, we saw a few pit bulls on a website for a shelter, and we made an appointment to meet them. But my wife's dog didn't like any of the pit bulls.

Then the guy at the shelter brought out what he called a pit-bull mix. I didn't like her at all. I thought to myself, "That dog looks like she is 1% pit bull."

The first thing our dog did was pee on the pit bull mix. I laughed, thinking that our dog didn't like the pit bull mix, but the worker said that was a good sign. He was right. The two of them started running around and playing with one another. I rolled my eyes and agreed to adopt that pit-bull mix.

"After all, we can always bring her back," I told my wife.

She looked at me as if I had just told her I was having an affair.

A few nights after the new dog came to live with us, I was working late, and by the time I came to bed, I saw the new dog sleeping in our bed. She was snoring just like my old dog used to do. That melted my heart.

But she was sleeping in my space, so I put my arms around her to carry her to the foot of the bed. She growled at me and tried to bite my arm.

I jumped back, scared, but then I got mad and started screaming at her. "Oh, hell no! Get out! Get out!" The dog ran to her crate and spent the rest of the night there.

The next day, I was sitting on the sofa watching TV. I had kept my distance from the new dog because I was still mad at her, but then she jumped next to me and cuddled up on my lap. Again, my heart melted right away, especially after she started to take and eat pieces of the apple I was eating, just like my old dog used to do.

"Ok, maybe I scared you when I tried to pick you up that night," I told the dog while I patted her head. I picked her up from the sofa a couple of times. "See, I wasn't trying to hurt you, I just needed a bit of space."

That night, I was working late again and by the time I came to bed, the new dog was again sleeping on my side of the bed. This time I approached her slowly and talked to her. "I'm just going to move you a little bit."

I put my arms underneath her and started to pick her up. She looked at me and started to growl. I put her down immediately. I started screaming at her again. "Oh hell no! Get out! Get out!"

"What's going on?" my wife asked, waking up.

"She tried to bite me again, and now she won't move from my spot."

My wife got up and the dog immediately followed her out of the bedroom. We closed the door to keep her out.

The next morning, as I got ready to go to work, I felt something under my foot. I looked down to see that I had just stepped in dog poo.

I screamed, "Ahhhhh!"

It woke up my wife. "What's happened?" she asked.

I pointed at my foot.

"OK, she had accident," my wife said, going back to bed.

This didn't look like an accident to me. Every night that we kept the new dog away from the bed, she would leave accidents on the floor for me to step on.

Then I went out of town, and I came back late at night. I walked into the bedroom and saw the dog on the bed by my wife's feet.

I thought about picking her up, but I was too exhausted to start drama in the middle of the night. Plus, I had plenty of space on my side of the bed.

The next morning when I woke up, the dog was still in the bed and there were no accidents in the house. It suddenly hit me: she was giving me shit because I was giving her shit.

Before I left for work, I came back into the bedroom to give my wife a goodbye kiss. The dog looked at me, probably worried that I was going to kick her out, but I left her there. I had been missing my old dog so much that I wanted this new dog to act just like her. I needed to accept her for who she was, just like I wanted her to accept me for who I was.

LOST

"Have a good day," my wife said with a smile as she dropped me off at work.

I saw her drive away, and I got sad that I had to go to work while she had the day off. I felt even sadder because she was on her way to the park with our two dogs. And even sadder because it was raining and she was driving my brand-new car with our two dogs in it.

Goodbye new-car smell. Hello wet-dog smell.

I went to work and a couple of hours later, my phone started to ring.

I ignored my phone because I am not allowed to answer the phone at work.

A few minutes later my phone started ringing again. I looked at the phone. It was a call from my wife.

That was strange, because she knew that I was not allowed to answer the phone at work; she always texted me if she needed to talk to me.

The phone rang again.

Before I could answer it stopped ringing, and a text followed immediately: *I lost one of our dogs in the park.*

I picked up the phone and called my wife. I knew I was not allowed to, but I didn't want to work in a place where I lost a dog and they didn't think it was an emergency.

She explained how one of our dogs had seen something that caught his attention and pulled at the leash so hard that she couldn't hold it.

"You want me to get out of work?" I asked. I was worried for our dog. (But also looking for an excuse to get out of work early.)

"It won't do any good," my wife replied. "By now he could be anywhere."

She told me that she had been driving around looking for our dog. A park worker had seen him run down an alley, and my wife had followed, but she couldn't find him.

"I am going back home to make some fliers," my wife said.

I hung up the phone and started staring out the window. I couldn't help but think that our dog might walk back to where my wife had dropped me off earlier that day. Because he loves me and because I love our dog, for the next twenty minutes, I couldn't do anything but stare out the window hoping to see him out there.

After a few minutes I decided to make a post on Facebook about our lost dog.

I am not supposed to be on Facebook while at work, but I wasn't supposed to be on the phone either. I figured that if I was going to get in trouble for breaking a rule, I might as well break a few more.

I posted a picture of our dog, a note explaining he was lost, and my phone number, in case anyone saw him.

I continued looking out the window and then I started thinking: our dog has a chip, doesn't this chip have a GPS signal to track him? Since I hadn't broken enough rules, I called my wife to ask. But she explained that no, the chip only has contact information in case he got lost.

"Well, he is lost right now." All I could think was: the chip is not helping.

Half an hour later, my phone started ringing.

I didn't even check to see who was calling.

"Did you lose a dog?" the caller asked.

"Yes, yes," I answered. "My dog ran away from my wife."

The guy on the other side of the line started laughing. I guess it was funny to picture my dog trying to run away from my wife as if he was tired of living with her.

I asked the guy if he had seen my Facebook post.

He responded, "No."

It turns out that his wife was on her way to work when she had seen a dog walking around in the alley. She figured he was lost because he had a leash on. She opened the door of her car, the dog jumped in, and then she drove him to her house and left him in her yard.

She told her husband to keep an eye on the dog. He was about to go to the police station to report the dog when he got a call from a neighbor.

"That dog in your yard looks like a lost dog I saw on Facebook," the neighbor told him.

He didn't have a social media account, so his neighbor walked over to show him. That's when he decided to call me.

I said thank you, and I gave him my wife's information so he could contact her, so I wouldn't get in trouble for being on the phone.

Later the day, my wife came to my job in my brand-new car to pick me up. I was happy to get out of work, happier to see my wife, and even happier to see our two dogs in the car with her.

Everyone was smiling.

I got in my brand-new car, took a big breath, and that's when a horrible smell hit me.

"What's the smell?" I asked my wife.

"He lost a fight with a skunk," she replied.

I was sad that my car had lost its new-car smell.

But I was happy that my family was complete once again.

DEDICATION

Special thanks to the incarcerated individuals at Stateville Correctional Center that are part of our writers group every Saturday morning. I thank them for their feedback and edits to the first draft of this book.

To North Side Pets for their ever loving and expert care of our friends whenever work or other duties keep us away from home.

To Michael John Ferry for his expertise and patience (twice) at helping us find our forever home.

And finally thanks to all my family and friends for their love and support.

ABOUT TORTOISE BOOKS

Slow and steady wins in the end, even in publishing. Tortoise Books is dedicated to finding and promoting quality authors who haven't yet found a niche in the marketplace—writers producing memorable and engaging works that will stand the test of time.

Learn more at www.tortoisebooks.com or follow us on BlueSky @tortoisebooks.bsky.social.

ABOUT THE AUTHOR

Nestor "The Boss" Gomez was born in Guatemala and traveled to Chicago in the mid 80s. He was undocumented, stuttered, and didn't know English. He didn't have a voice. Today Nestor is an American citizen, speaks English with a sexy Latin accent, and has become a storyteller, winning nearly a hundred Moth Slams. He has found his voice.

He is the creator, producer, curator and host of *80 Minutes Around the World*, a storytelling show that features the stories of immigrants, their descendants, and allies. He is also the author of *Your Driver Has Arrived* and *Rescued Me.* To learn more about Nestor, visit his website: nestorgomezstoryteller.com

ABOUT THE COVER ARTIST

Andrés J. Colmenares is a cartoonist and illustrator, creator of Wawawiwa comics, a webcomic followed by millions of fans around the globe. He lives in Colombia.